The Power of Dreams

A History of Healing Body, Mind and Soul

By Francesco Ancona

DEDICATION

To my loving wife, the most enthusiastic of cheerleaders, who spiritedly spurred me on yet somehow always knew when to tiptoe quietly about—all my thanks and love!

And to my parents, who inspired me in life and presently encourage me in my dreams—I only wish I knew then to say thank you more and realize that I can never say thank you enough now.

ACKNOWLEDGEMENTS

Dr. Liana Piehler and Dr. Virginia Phelan for all of their hard work, inspiration, encouragement, and goodness. I am extremely grateful. Without your help, I would never have been able to complete this project.

The Power of Dreams:
A History of Healing Body, Mind,and Soul
by Dr. Francesco Ancona

Library of Congress Control Number:
2015953044
ISBN 978-1-55605-464-8

EBook Version 978-1-55605-465-5

Wyndham Hall Press
5050 Kerr Rd.
Lima, OH 45806

Contents

Chapter One

INTRODUCTION

We all dream, and we are all mystified and often perplexed or even overwhelmed by the enigmatic narratives of our nightly journeys— which we create, in which we star, and which we observe as bewildered and enthralled yet captive audiences. Just as the ebony plum blue sky twinkles with dazzling stars, the darkness of sleep is illuminated by the richness of our dreams. Like the hopes, fears, and fancies of children wishing upon shooting stars, in our dreams, anything and everything is possible: We fly, confront the most frightening of monsters, inherit millions, or even witness our own deaths. Indeed, dreams are nocturnal miracles. Sadly, however, few realize how much these miracles are essential for the health of our bodies, minds, and souls.

Indeed, dreams are the most misunderstood necessity of life. The needs for shelter, food, water, and air are all clearly recognized and valued, but the immeasurable importance of dreams is too often overlooked. However, without dreams our species would not survive. Over the vast millennia of human development, nature has perfected the "ideal survival paradigm": dreaming. Hence, it is imperative to recognize the importance of dreams and to understand how they function to affect the physical, mental, and spiritual health of each individual as well as of the human race itself. For ironically, dreams "awaken" us to the truth and wholeness of our very being.

To help bring to light the magic of dreams, the following chapters survey the separate areas of dream studies to unify as well as confirm the tripartite physical, mental, and spiritual nature of dreams from what the ancients knew to contemporary scientific discoveries because such an inclusive, multicultural, multidisciplinary approach is necessary to redress the compartmentalization in any therapeutic field of research inherently subject to overspecialization. Additionally, this undertaking is a "vision quest" of sorts. Its interdisciplinary perspective, whereby the whole is revealed to be "more than the sum of its parts," is an individual yet collective journey to truth. To each person, the question—Who am I?—can be answered on a personal level through her or his dreams. Dreams reveal each unique personality, address bodily as well as mental health issues, and awaken emotions. And as importantly, the larger spiritual question—the greatest of all enigmas—what happens to the soul (if it even exists) after death can also be explored through the otherworldly travels of our dreams. Through the "great" collective dreams, we are connected to what Carl Gustav Jung identified as our eternal and truer selves.

First, on the somatic level, regarding matters of health, sleep and dreams help regulate the complexity of systems that inform and govern our bodies; for example, dream/sleep disorders are currently recognized as contributing factors in hypertension and obesity, specifically causing insulin resistance and impaired glucose tolerance. And sleep deprivation—especially in regards to its disruption of dream cycles—is a cause of fatigue-related accidents and clinical/workplace errors. Furthermore, the lack of proper sleep and dreaming negatively impacts mood and memory and increases the use and abuse of alcohol and other stimulants. Additionally, sleep disorders, like obstructive apnea, are underlying mechanisms for heart failure, stroke, and coronary artery disease. In fact, recent research is also revealing a correlation of sleep/dream disturbances to alterations in genetic morbidity, specifically impeding one's longevity.

However, because increasing numbers of contemporary neurological researchers are focusing on primarily the negative health impacts of sleep disorders and deprivation, it is vitally important here to also recognize the all-important interrelationship of sleep and dreams to avoid any isolation of sleep studies that ignores the importance of dreaming. The very nature and, most likely, purpose of sleep is "perchance to dream." Therefore, exploring the importance of dreams to effecting physical, mental, and spiritual health illustrates the necessity of harmonizing these key elements, so they work together to foster better, healthier lives.

For example, dreams should be recognized for their diagnostic qualities, for instance Prodromal dreams can predict pregnancy before any current technology, and they can alert individuals to disease and medical conditions. Furthermore, dreams can help pharmacologists to determine patient states of mood and, thereby, clarify and facilitate the sometimes difficult decision of how much and when to dispense certain narcotic and psychotic prescriptions. Nevertheless, the role of dreaming is much more important than simply bridging unconscious awareness to somatic processes. The sleep and dream cycles essential to preserving life are now understood to function as "brain washers" so to speak, because they "flush" potentially neurotoxic waste products from the central nervous system and, thereby, help ensure metabolic homeostasis.

These recent physiological research findings are important because they recognize the all-important body-mind relationship and reinforce the complementary functioning of somatic and mental health systems. This is especially evident in the latest treatments for Posttraumatic Stress Disorder (PTSD), which successfully combine pharmacological and analytical therapies.

Second, the potential of dreams to effect mental health has been recognized since even before the dawn of history. Prehistoric cave art and artifacts reveal a human identification with deity, the Goddess, specifically acknowledging the relationship of the perishable individual, mortal self, to eternal wholeness. The importance of dreams has been preserved over the millennia, and evidence of this safeguarding is also readily discernible in the earliest of historical records that outline dream interpretation techniques to soothe the individual psyche as well as to reconnect it with the universal source of mental stability and wellbeing.

Moreover, modern dream analysts, beginning with the seminal works of Sigmund Freud and Carl Gustav Jung, have brought forth a renaissance of personal and collective dream interpretation methodologies. *Gestalt* psychology, for example, uses dreams to redress the "holes" in our psyches to make us "whole" once again, and phenomenology seeks to illuminate the self by removing the mental blockages to the true light of our unconscious. Today, this "golden age" is being furthered by contemporary analysts, whose therapeutic techniques are essential to effect mental health for individuals and societies in this ever changing, fast-paced world. The "monsters" we confront now are not only physical but also mental. Therefore, in many ways, they are far more complex than the simple beasts that stalked our prehistoric ancestors, for they are far more invisible and, subsequently, more damaging. As a result, we need our dreams to help defeat our demons. As researchers are currently proving, during non-REM sleep we formulate strategies to conquer our haunting fears, then rehearse these strategies during REM sleep, where the worst consequence we face for failed plans is to simply awaken.

Third, on a spiritual level, dreams identify us with the birthplace of all life; they connect us to the fount of ultimate wisdom through which we come to realize our "oneness" with all humanity as well as with the source from which we gain infinite knowledge of the great mystery that structures and informs us all. From the prehistoric caves through the earliest historical periods to this contemporary world, the importance of dreams as conduits to our souls has been recognized over and over again. The shapes and forms of deities may change, but that immortal radicle, that creator of the roots of "being," remains the same—especially visible to us in our dreams.

Thus, spiritual dreams are "living mythologies." They are "intimations of immortality," important to effecting and restoring spiritual health in a contemporary culture of ever increasing isolation and its resultant dissolution and dehumanization of not only the individual, but also of all humanity.

Ultimately, comprehending the triune physical, mental, and spiritual healing nature of dreams is like trying to contain the shape-shifting Proteus who, only after being firmly embraced, will reveal his boon: "truth." This is why a knowledge and understanding of all three therapeutic functions of dreams must be simultaneously held in one's body, mind, and soul. For it is only through this Protean perspective—this all inclusive relationship—that the three can become one in a trinity of healing.

Chapter Two

DREAMS AND MENTAL HEALTH

On the occasion of his seventieth birthday, Sigmund Freud confessed, "The poets and philosophers before me discovered the unconscious." Then he added, "What I discovered was the scientific method by which the unconscious can be studied."[1] Although there are many who would prefer to classify Freud himself as a philosopher and dispute his insistence on defining psychoanalysis as a "science," most would admit that Freud was quite correct to acknowledge his debt to "poets and philosophers," especially the earliest of them. So much of what Freud defines as the "dream-work,"[2] a Rosetta Stone of sorts to make intelligible the enigmatic symbolism of dreams, is to be found in the theories of our earliest ancestors.

What the Ancients Knew

Readily discernable elements of prehistoric dream representation, chiefly of a spiritual nature, appear in the cave art, carvings, and artifacts of our earliest progenitors.[3] But the historical period is problematic since it is very difficult to pinpoint exactly when and where dream interpretation and its role in effecting mental health first appear because the dates of the original oral sources of existing written remnants are unknown. As J. Donald Hughes explains:

> It is difficult to say just which mention of dream interpretation is the oldest, but ancient Sumeria seems to hold precedence. The dreams of Gilgamesh (c. 2700-2600 B. C.), king of the Sumerian city of Uruk, are recorded in the epic that bears his name, but this is a literary work and our oldest fragments do not go back beyond 2000 B. C.[4] Hughes concludes,

"Gilgamesh is a historian's gold mine of dreams of different types."[5]

However, Curtiss Hoffman refutes Hughes' assertion and presents an earlier sample of an ancient Mesopotamian dream text, that of Dumuzi, whose "name appears in the Sumerian King List as king of the city of Uruk just before that of the more famous Gilgamesh."[6] The Dumuzi text is believed to date from about 1800-1700 B.C.E., but derived from a much earlier oral source. It is part of the larger epic entitled *Descent of Inanna*, which includes both Dumuzi's dream and his sister Geshtin-anna's interpretation of it, an interpretation that helps reveal a lot about Mesopotamian culture.[7] This approach, whereby the individual psyche is recognized in terms of identification with one's culture, is also evidenced in ancient Egyptian dream interpretations, the origin of which may also be traced to the second millennium B.C.E.

Nevertheless, regardless of the origin of the earliest surviving documents, dreams in antiquity, as Hughes asserts, were often interpreted by "Wise Ones," as for example Geshtin-anna, who is believed to have been a professional dream interpreter: " Symbolic dreams required interpretation, and judging from the extant texts, were never analyzed by the dreamer alone. Most commonly, a wise person was consulted: a god, goddess, priest, priestess, courtier, physician, professional dream interpreter, relative, or friend."[8]

This reliance on "experts" is one of the initial cornerstones[9] of Freudian psychoanalysis. However, by no means is it the only instance of ancient dream interpretation principles predating modern psychoanalytic ideas. For example, the Egyptian Chester Beatty papyrus[10] provides for interpreting images by their opposites, using colloquial Egyptian word and image puns. More specifically, this papyrus' identification of what analysts today term "reaction formation," whereby something is turned into its opposite, is an early recognition of a very complex psychoanalytical process, which Nancy McWilliams outlines: "The defense of *reaction formation* is an intriguing phenomenon. Evidently, the human organism is capable of turning something into its polar opposite in order to render it less threatening. The traditional definition of reaction formation involves this conversion of a negative into a positive affect or vice versa. The transformation of hatred into love, or longing into contempt, or envy into attraction, for example, can be inferred from many common transactions."[11]

As McWilliams further explains, the psychic mechanism of reaction formation is a difficult but important process to help understand the structural components of human mental states: "A more accurate way to depict reaction formation than as the turning of an emotion into its opposite might be to note that it functions to deny ambivalence. It is a basic psychoanalytic assumption that no disposition is totally unmixed. We can hate the person we love or resent the person to whom we feel grateful; our emotional situation does not simply reduce to one or the other positions."[12]

Thus, the ancient Egyptian papyrus is a primitive recognition of a complex psychological defense mechanism through which one's dream proves to be an effort to persuade one's self, "that all that is felt is one polarity of a complex emotional response,"[13] in order to reduce the intense psychic pain of wallowing in ambivalence.

Additionally, the Egyptians as well as the Sumerians believed that through such an interpretive system as outlined in the Chester Beatty papyrus, dreams could be incubated[14] to ward off nightmares or solve mind-boggling waking dilemmas. Once the enigma is resolved through a process reminiscent of Freudian psychoanalysis, where the analyst sits at the head of the analysand and "shares" the dreaming experience via the process of transference, the dreamer can find relief, usually in ancient Egypt through acclimation to her/his culture: "...[T]he vocabularies of both the Sumerian and Akkadian languages, as spoken in the third melennium [sic] B.C., contain a term (LU.SAG.SHE.NA = mu-pa-shir) that means "one who sleeps beside (or at the head of) another person" – "one who does the interpretation of dreams." This was in all probability a priest or priestess whose purpose was to have a dream that would help the inquirer to understand his or her own dreams."[15]

In Egypt as in Mesopotamia, dreams were usually interpreted through a cultural lens. However, although it can be strongly argued that Egypt was the origin of Classical Greek dream interpretation practices, in the migration, the way in which dreams were interpreted appears to have changed from a cultural (Egyptian) to an individual (Grecian) process of analysis. Gregory Shushan compared Egyptian and Greek dreams in the archives of two Ptolemaic second-century B.C.E. writers. The first archive was that of Ptolemaios, a Greek recluse in the temple of Astarte; the second archive belonged to Hor, an Egyptian scribe and priest in the temples of Isis and Thoth. Shushan concludes: "Overall, the cultural level is most evident in Hor's dreams which contain typically Egyptian images and themes similar to Egyptian literary and magical texts and dream-books. In contrast, the dreams in Ptolemaios' archive contain more prominent personal levels, reflecting the struggles and concerns of daily life."[16] This shift from cultural to personal dream interpretation is evident in the processes utilized in the Greek Asclepieia.

In ancient Greece, the Asclepieia, the most famous of which is Epidarus circa the fifth century B.C.E., are renowned for harnessing the healing nature of dreams. Pilgrims would flock to an Asclepieion, where they participated in a process of dream incubation. They would sleep in the sanctuary amid snakes, a prehistoric symbol long associated with the healing profession and the emblem of Asclepius' healing powers.[17] Upon awakening, they would relate their dreams to the priests and priestesses, who would guide them in their curative efforts. Surviving plaques testify to the success of these temples, most likely due to the psychological concept inherent in the "placebo effect." As Cilliers and Retief point out: "The readiness and susceptibility of the patients in the Asclepieia when going to sleep have already been pointed out: their preoccupation with their suffering, the sight of the *iamata*[18] and the statue of the god himself in his temple, and their fervent expectation of and belief in their healing—all of this would have prepared them emotionally and fine-tuned them, as it were, to react positively on any suggestion."[19]

This ancient process of personal dream incubation predates a number of contemporary techniques—for example the role of self-hypnosis and the problem-solving nature of nonREM and REM sleep—as does Plato's recognition of the origin of dreams as expressions of buried adolescent emotions. To Plato, dreams could be repressed wishes, instinctual releases of the beasts within and in need of rational interpretation.

Other examples of how ancient philosophers predate the theories of Freud include the work of Artemidorus Daldianus Ephesius, a second century A.D. diviner,[20] who completed a five volume work, the *Oneirocritica* (*The Interpretation of Dreams*). In the *Oneirocritica*, Artemidorus recognized, as did Freud, the connection of day activities to nightly dreams; he also discussed the body-mind connection. As Christine Walde explains:

> In Artemidorus' fivefold classification, dreams manifesting the current status of body and frame of mind—especially fears, wishes, and digestion—fall into the category of *enhypnia.* In all ancient classifications of dreams, *enhypnia* are a difficult category as they include dreams of different causation—body and soul, psychological and physiological, and "day residues." Their common denominator is "temporal" and "ephemeral," as they show a direct and immediate connection to the dreamer and his waking life.[21]

A rudimentary psychological understanding of dreams also finds early expression in the ancient Vedas, the oral origins of which can be traced to somewhere in the fifteenth century B.C.E. In Hindu India, the identification of the gods as projections of human unconscious components can be recognized in the connection of dreams to individual "personality types":

As Raymond De Becker points out in his wonderfully informative book *The Understanding of Dreams*, the *Treatise* [*Treatise on Dreams* in the Atharva Veda] contains nothing like a modern method of dreams analysis, which focuses on the unique history and psychological structure of each individual. But, "it does contain a remarkable attempt to interpret images with reference to the personality, or at least the temperament, of the dreamer." The Indians at the time recognized three temperaments: the bilious, the phlegmatic, and the sanguine. The *Treatise* taught that these types could be recognized by their dream imagery. The imagery of a particular type could, in part, be predicted by the type of dreamer. According to De Becker, this is the first systematic effort to relate dream images to the physiological roots, thus ridding dreams of some of their magical trappings. Here we have perhaps the earliest expression of the belief in the physiological causes of dreams, which we shall refer to as the *physiological reality* of dreams. Because the conception of temperaments was not entirely physiological, but was considered a description of personality type as well, this may also be the earliest written account of the belief in the *psychological reality* of dreams as they pertained to the individual dreamer's personality type, not just to his future.[22]

Other cultures normally not generally recognized for their focus on the psychological nature of dreams do, nevertheless, display an understanding of their content as projections of mental processes. For example, early Jewish interpretations commonly focused on dreams as literal messages from God; however, their metaphorical nature should not be overlooked because of this spiritual emphasis. As Gayle Delaney asserts: "It may be that since dreams of spiritual encounters with God make such exciting, convincing, and educational reading for a large audience, the more personal, psychological dream work that may have been common was not included in most holy scriptures."[23] To demonstrate, Delaney cites Joseph's dream in which the sun, moon, and eleven stars all bow before him as metaphorical illustration of his unconscious desire as the youngest son to have his father, mother, and many brothers demonstrate visible obeisance to him.

In China, the earliest historical references to dreams reportedly occur during the Confucian age (fifth century B.C.E.); consequently, there is a strong connection of dreams to functioning in a social context. However, in the mid-second century A.D., Wang Fu identified ten categories of dreams, including those that reveal individual temperament and problem solving efforts.[24] The *Lie-Tseu*, a Taoist[25] dream book, also illustrates the psychological aspect of dreaming; from an interesting Freudian perspective, it provides:

>...[A] coherent theory of dreaming, and looks more specifically into the causes of dreams, teaching that waking wishes, illness, or environmentally caused somatic discomfort can cause dreams. The *Lie-Tseu* teaches that understanding of the causes of a dream will destroy the fear of the dream, if not its effects. This idea, later espoused by Freud, was probably not recognized by many interpreters, but "it was inherent in the Taoist philosophy, which held that mental troubles, whether of the day or the night, could be reduced by knowing their causes."[26]

Ultimately, even a precursory glance at what the ancients knew about dreams and mental health demonstrates that Freud was quite right to recognize his debt to philosophers and poets. But what about the debt contemporary oneirologists (dream enthusiasts) owe to the "Golden Age" of dream interpretation ushered in by the publication of Freud's *The Interpretation of Dreams*?

Modern/Contemporary Oneirology

Sigmund Freud

In modern times, dream interpretation by mental health practitioners flourished with the emergence of psychoanalysis at the brink of the twentieth century,[27] specifically with Sigmund Freud's *The Interpretation of Dreams.*

Until Freud's investigations in the last decade of the nineteenth century, dreams had been largely neglected as an object of serious scientific study and one may add, rightly so, since before him there was no adequate technique for studying them, with the result that whatever serious studies had been made of them had shed but little light upon them. It was his discovery of the psychoanalytic method that enabled Freud to discover more about dreams than it had been possible for any of his predecessors to learn.[28]

Whatever one may think of the theories of Sigmund Freud, the immense importance of *The Interpretation of Dreams* cannot be denied or overvalued. Succinctly, it is the germinal, definitive text in the field of dream interpretation, despite the fact that two of Freud's central theories have since been disproven: his assertion that dreams are wish fulfillments[29] and his supposition that we have a conscious censor scrambling their messages.

In explanation, it is important to note here that Freud was a "pioneer" forging ahead through unchartered waters; as a result, many of his theories were constantly changing as he modified and enlarged upon his earlier thoughts and experiences. For example, Freud himself recognized the limitations of his wish fulfillment theory and addressed them in *Beyond the Pleasure Principle,*[30] where he posited that, just like children who love to have the same story read to them, we also crave the ability to re-experience even our most frightening nightmares because we have two primal drives: Eros and Thanatos, the life and death desires. As long as we are alive (as the Buddha also concluded), all life is sorrowful; thus, we seek to return to a stasis state (death), which is the cessation of unpleasant experiences. Therefore, Freud surmised that the repetition of painful occurrences, especially near-death recollections like the nightmares of war veterans, were actually satisfactions of the wish to return to the death state in order to end, as Hamlet so aptly phrases it, "the slings and arrows of outrageous fortune" (3.1.59).[31] Hamlet also illustrates Freud's theory by his desire to escape the painful sufferings of his tortured self, "Oh, that this too too sullied flesh would melt,/Thaw, and resolve itself into a dew" (1.2.129-31)![32]

Ultimately, no matter how strained and perhaps mistaken they may prove to be, Freud's contributions to the understanding of dreams far outweigh the flaws in his pioneering efforts. His recognition of the existence of an unconscious and his creation of a "vocabulary" to discuss the language of dreams are two of the central tenets of dream interpretation. First, Freud recognized the functioning of an "unconscious" at work in dreams. As Brenner explains:

> Such a demonstration is important in itself, and can be made without any special technique of observation. However, by means of the psychoanalytic technique, Freud was able to demonstrate that behind *every* dream there are active unconscious thoughts and desires, and thus to establish as a *general rule* that when dreams occur they are caused by mental activity which is unconscious to the dreamer, and which would remain so without the use of the psychoanalytic technique.[33]

Second, in order to understand the metaphorical language of the unconscious as revealed in dreams, Freud outlined a system of methodologies to translate the symbolic nature of dream images: "The dream-thoughts we can understand without further trouble the moment we have ascertained them. The dream-content is, as it were, presented in hieroglyphics, whose symbols must be translated, one by one, in the language of the dream-thoughts. It would, of course, be incorrect to attempt to read these symbols in accordance with their values as pictures, instead of in accordance with their meaning as symbols."[34]

Freud termed the vocabulary of this Rosetta Stone of the unconscious the "dream-work":

> I have given the name of *dream-work* to the process which, with the cooperation of the censorship, converts the latent thoughts

into the manifest content of the dream. It consists of a peculiar way of treating the preconscious material of thought, so that its component parts become *condensed*, its psychical emphasis becomes *displaced*, and the whole of it is translated into visual images or *dramatized*, and completed by a deceptive *secondary revision*. The dream-work is an excellent example of the processes occurring in the deeper, unconscious layers of the mind, which differ considerably from the familiar normal process of thought. It also displays a number of archaic characteristics, such as the use of a *symbolism*…which it has since also been possible to discover in other spheres of mental activity.[35]

Freud posited the existence of two different "languages" speaking simultaneously in dreams. The manifest dream thought, solely on which prior interpretation efforts focused, was the basic narrative of the dream, its plot. The "latent dream-content" was a completely different language, emanating from the unconscious "id" and relating its theme through symbolism. It is essential for an analyst to understand the latent dream-content because, try as one might to avoid facing one's fears and repressions, an analysand (a psychoanalytic patient) will eventually reveal the true workings of his/her unconscious through dreams:

> Freud made the simple but penetrating observation that if a dreamer is encouraged to go on talking about his dream images and the thoughts that these prompt in his mind, he will give himself away and reveal the unconscious background of his ailments, in both what he says and what he deliberately omits saying. His ideas may seem irrational and irrelevant, but after a time it becomes relatively easy to see what it is that he is trying to avoid, what unpleasant thought or experience he is suppressing. No matter how he tries to camouflage it, everything he says points to the core of his predicament.[36]

In order to translate the symbolic, enigmatic imagery of dreams into an intelligible system of manifest thought, Freud outlined a number of processes that make up the dream-work, beginning with condensation and displacement and including projection, representation, and elaboration.

Condensation

Freud realized that the dream-content—the narrative, plot, or storyline—is relatively short in comparison to its analysis; therefore, he explained this disparity by concluding, "The fact...is irrefutable that dream-formation is based on a process of dream condensation."[37] As a result, even a short dream adequately described in a paragraph or two could require an analysis that might fill many pages because, through the process of condensation, each image reveals itself to have a multitude of meanings. It is as if each dream image were similar to a tiny circus car rolling onto center ring; suddenly, its doors and roof fly open almost magically, freeing numerous large clowns carrying bunches of balloons and buckets of confetti to toss at the awed crowd. Condensation packs into each dream image a variety of meanings, some even contradictory in nature.[38]

Perhaps a different way to understand condensation is through an example from the field of Quantum Physics. Thanks to the enormity of the latest cyclotrons, scientists are discovering astonishing reactions when atoms are crashed into each other at enormous speeds. Contrary to reasonable expectations, when atoms collide, they do not simply break up as expected into their observable pieces; rather, they release unexpected, unimagined elements. To illustrate, if one were to crash a Volkswagen into a Toyota, the cars would rupture into pieces of Volkswagen and Toyota. However, this is not the case when atoms collide. Out of the Volkswagen and Toyota collision could come Fords and fire engines, pick-up trucks, Hondas and ambulances. In like manner, through the process of condensation, one dream image could release a multitude of unexpected and almost incomprehensible meanings, including those in absolute opposition with each other.

Nevertheless, as inexplicable as these dream images may appear, there is a proverbial method to their madness, as one of my dreams may help to explain. Immediately upon graduation from high school, I was drafted into the Army. Like most teenagers, I had a high school sweetheart. But my deployment soon resulted in a "Dear John" letter from (let us call her) "Nicole," letting me know that we were no longer dating. One can imagine the multitude of different emotions I was feeling, ranging from sadness, frustration, and helplessness to anger and a number of feelings of which I wasn't even consciously aware. A couple of years later, when I returned home after completing my tour of duty, I serendipitously ran into Nicole while we were both doing grocery shopping at a local supermarket. She was standing at the back of the market. Anxious to recapture our relationship, I ran over to her and tried to convince her to go out on a date. However, she was very cold to the idea but after a lot of persistence on my behalf, she finally and as I could observe reluctantly agreed. "I'd be happy," she said, "if you would just meet me for lunch."

Needless to say, I was ecstatic and couldn't wait to see her, but the night before we were to meet, I had this dream: I was sitting patiently in the restaurant waiting for Nicole. Even though it was a bright sunny day, the restaurant was dimly lit by flickering candles set on checkered tablecloths. I was sipping some wine and listening to soft, romantic music playing in the background but getting anxious because she was very late. Just as I was about to leave, however, the door opened in a burst of bright sunlight that silhouetted Nicole as she entered, making her appear almost angelic. She wore a lovely floral print summer dress and curiously, for she never wore them in waking life, a tight string of pearls were fashioned around her neck. I wanted very much to please her, so as she approached the table, I rose in a gentlemanly manner to pull out her chair. However, rather than help her to be seated, I lifted her up and put her into a meat grinder. I woke up in absolute panic! How could I even have had such a dream?

The meaning can be revealed through the process of condensation. The central image of Nicole in the meat grinder is a "nodal point." This one image is like the circus car filled with clowns. It holds numerous, unexpected meanings—some of which are opposite to others. It recreates the multitude of diverse emotions I felt years earlier when Nicole sent me that "break-up" letter. Without going too deeply into the imagery, it obviously displays anger and a need for revenge. But simultaneously, it also illustrates my desire to make her happy and to get her back again. First, my resentment of Nicole stemmed from her treatment of me as less than human, as figuratively "a piece of meat." This is echoed by the setting of the chance encounter that triggered the dream, the back of a supermarket where meats are kept refrigerated. Unknowingly, my unconscious was associating Nicole with the products of the meat freezers behind her.

Second, in a curious twist of language, it also reflects my desire to make Nicole happy. Remember, she said that it would make her happy if I would "meet her" for lunch. The image of Nicole in the meat grinder is a rebus in which the phrase "meet me for lunch" is presented in pictorial format as "meat me for lunch," thereby satisfying her request. Similarly, the tight string of pearls which she never wore in waking life is also a rebus of sorts, this time to illustrate my repressed anger as such a necklace is called a "choker." Thus, through an understanding of the process of condensation, it is easy to recognize how one dream image can communicate by recreating a wealth of hidden meanings and repressed emotional states.

Displacement

Ironically, the source of one's mental anguish may not actually appear in the dream content; rather, because of its painful nature, it may only be hinted at or be positioned in the background. According to

Freud: "That which is obviously the essential content of the dream-thoughts need not be represented at all in the dream. The dream is, as it were, *centered elsewhere*; its content is arranged about elements which do not constitute the central point of the dream-thoughts."[39]

However, unlike the complicated concept of dream condensation, dream displacement can be readily understandable in general, lay terms. Recognizing the proximity of technical psychoanalytical interpretation and the general understanding of displacement as a defense mechanism, McWilliams explains: "*Displacement* is…popularly appreciated without much distortion of its technical psychoanalytic meaning… The term displacement refers to the redirection of a drive, emotion, preoccupation, or behavior from its initial or natural object to another because its original direction is for some reason anxiety ridden."[40]

For example, because of the love/hate ambivalence in a father/son relationship, a father may be angry at his son but not wish to express that anger in fear of further stressing their fragile bond, so he dreams that his next door neighbor punishes the boy for some similar or even unrelated transgression. Hence, through the process of displacement, the father's anger at his son is expressed and released; however, because it is "displaced" onto someone else and/or expressed in dissimilar fashion, the release of that anger does not create an excess of anxiety or a backlash of guilt in the father, himself.

Projection

Similar to displacement, the process of projection allows dreamers to ascribe (project) their fantasies onto others, again in an effort to express and release the painful repression without suffering the resultant guilt and anxiety. Freud recognized projection as a defense mechanism which functions to minimize the painful ambivalence of one's actions, especially those actions which would inflict suffering on others.[41] As a teacher, I experience the process of projection daily in the explosive reaction of failing students, who never blame themselves; rather, they project their failures onto teachers, parents, the school, the course, and even their textbooks.

Ultimately, projection is an important process because it reveals the connection between dream interpretation and healing, for it is only through recognition of the ambivalent nature of the original cause of one's mental anguish that one can affect any hope of a cure. Dreams reveal the ambivalence behind our consciously repressed emotions, for example, in the case of the death of one who has provoked such "double feeling":

The double feeling—tenderness and hostility—against the deceased, which we consider well founded, endeavours to assert itself at the time of bereavement as mourning and satisfaction. A conflict must ensue between these contrary feelings, and as one of them, namely the hostility, is altogether or for the greater part unconscious, the conflict cannot result in a conscious difference in the form of hostility or tenderness as, for instance, when we forgive an injury inflicted upon us by someone we love. This process usually adjusts itself through a special psychic mechanism, which is designated in psychoanalysis as *projection*. This unknown hostility, of which we are ignorant and of which we do not wish to know, is projected from our inner perception into the outer world and is thereby detached from our own person and attributed to the other. Not we, the survivors, rejoice because we are rid of the deceased, on the contrary, we mourn for him; but now, curiously enough, he has become an evil demon who would rejoice in our misfortune and who seeks our death. The survivors must now defend themselves against this evil enemy; they are free from inner oppression, but they have only succeeded in exchanging it for an affliction from without.[42]

Dreams safely allow us to recognize this ambivalence; such recognition is the important first step towards reducing the psychic pain and confusion caused by the guilty repression of the perplexing agony of our "double feelings."

Representation

Because the "language" of dreams is primarily pictorial, the waking life use of words to create relationships between and among ideas is not usually presented. A dream, like the processes of painting and sculpture, does not often utilize conjunctions like "and" to relate messages of equality, or does it use terms like "as" or "like" to communicate similarities or "because" to portray causal relationships between ideas. As Freud recognized, "To begin with, we must answer that the dream has at its disposal no means of representing...logical relationships between the dream-thoughts."[43] As a result, in its place, the nonverbal, pictographic process of representation is used to demonstrate relationships between and among dream elements. For instance, a person in a dream could begin as a particular individual but then change into someone else. Similarly, a dream can begin in one locale but shift suddenly to another or be situated in a very familiar locale that does not seem to be itself, thereby communicating the cause and effect nature of the juxtaposition of images. The first part of the dream can be perceived as causing the resultant second half of the dream. For example, if one were to dream of oneself as a hideous clown being laughed at by a ridiculing audience then find oneself in the same dream inexplicably driving a car into an embankment, the message could be that one's negative self-image (as depicted by the grotesque clown in the first part of the dream) is causing one's life to crash senselessly as is the car in the second half of the dream.

Another example of dream representation could be the blending of two different images melding into one. To illustrate, I once had a dream of my late grandmother as the race horse Sea Biscuit. In this instance, my dream was trying to communicate a relationship of equality:

Both were "underdogs" yet despite the enormous odds against them, they both achieved greatness. Despite being a single mom and a newly arrived immigrant who did not speak English, my grandmother somehow managed to support and feed her three children on her own. Once I recognized this equivalency, the representation presented in this dream helped me heal through a difficult time of mental anguish, when I sincerely doubted my ability to complete my doctorate. I had already accrued a lot of tuition debt and was unemployed. Additionally, I was overwhelmed by the prospect of writing a book length dissertation. I was worried, frightened, and ready to quit. So this dream functioned to remind me of the "thoroughbred" bloodline that I had inherited from my grandmother and woke me to the realization that despite all odds, I, too, could be a winner like Sea Biscuit and her. In my case, I could successfully cross the finish line by not giving up and completing the requirements of my degree.

Elaboration

The conscious mind becomes uncomfortably perplexed by, and in reaction to, the enigmatic nature of the latent dream meaning because it desires to have all the proverbial "i's" dotted and all the "t's" crossed; consequently, it relieves the anxiety of confronting the bewildering and unsatisfying dream pictures by inserting any and all imagined pieces, no matter how erroneously they may be applied, to complete the confounding puzzle. In this way, elaboration can become a defense mechanism that allows for the dream to be understood through the images the waking mind chooses to add to it, thus releasing the stress of having to confront uncontrolled messages from the unconscious, thereby concretizing the dream and transforming it from a metaphorical construct to a literal portrayal.[44] Through the insertion of nonthreatening material, the waking mind neutralizes any uncomfortably puzzling unconscious dream elements.

From this perspective, elaboration can be readily recognized as problematic to the process of mental healing as it negates or distorts important dream revelations. To paraphrase the Peace Corps slogan, "If you're not part of the cure, you're part of the problem." Fortunately, these conscious falsehoods, like all "little white lies," recede with time. Consequently, it is important to keep a dream diary to create a benchmark for contrasting one's later recollection of initially recorded dreams. Any forgotten elements from the original dream diary omitted upon reiteration are most likely products of elaboration and can be, for the most part, safely disregarded—very much like the awareness and deletion of unimportant elements a writer omits during her/his revision processes.

Ultimately, by awakening us to the existence and functioning of the unconscious and providing a language with which we can discuss our repressions, desires and defenses, Freud's contribution to the study of dreams and their potential to effect mental health make him not only the "pioneering" dream analyst but also one of the most influential, quintessential, and esteemed.

> Freud's [*The*] *Interpretation of Dreams* is about more than dreams... [I]t offers a survey of fundamental psychoanalytic ideas—the Oedipus complex, the work of repression, the struggle between desire and defense—and a wealth of material from case histories... It opens with an exhaustive bibliographical survey of the literature on dreams, and it concludes, in the difficult seventh chapter, with a comprehensive theory of the mind. The genre of Freud's masterpiece is, in short, undefinable.[45]

Carl Gustav Jung

Originally considered by Sigmund Freud to be his "heir apparent," Carl Gustav Jung rebelled against his figurative "father" and is now recognized on his own merits as one of the giants, if not *the* giant, of dream analysis. Basically, there were two major reasons for Jung's dissention: First, Freud envisioned psychoanalysis in scientific terms;

that is, he wanted to avoid attaching the stigma of philosophy or, even more importantly, religion to his "new science." Second, although Jung accepted Freud's theory of a personal unconscious composed of repressed sufferings and unfulfilled desires, he believed it was incomplete. To Jung, there are actually four levels of the psyche: personal consciousness (everyday awareness); personal unconscious (unique to the individual); objective psyche[46] (collective, universal to all humankind); and collective consciousness (cultural world of shared values/forms).[47] Consequently, to Jung dreams could be personal or collective, and as such they could contain a multitude of shared symbolism, which he called "archetypes." These archetypes are universally inherited projections of the collective unconscious. Jung explains the distinction between learned and inherent psychic content, "Whereas the contents of the *personal unconscious* are acquired during the individual's lifetime, the contents of the *collective unconscious* are invariably archetypes that were present from the beginning."[48] Those from the collective unconscious, especially the shadow and anima/animus, "have the most frequent and the most disturbing influence on the ego."[49]

Before discussing the archetypes of the collective unconscious as they manifest in dreams, I will present an overview of their role in the process of "individuation" to clarify their function as essential elements in the quest to effect mental health. As M.-L.von Franz explains: "By observing a great many people and studying their dreams (he estimated that he interpreted at least 80,000 dreams), Jung discovered not only that all dreams are relevant in varying degrees to the life of the dreamer, but that they are all parts of one great web of psychological factors. He also found that, on the whole, they seem to follow an arrangement or pattern. This pattern Jung called 'the process of individuation.'"[50]

Initially, an individual begins life as an "undifferentiated whole"; however, as one lives, one experiences a constant process of differentiation: The cell divides, developing into a fetus; the fetus is separated from the womb; and so on. Eventually, ...[J]ust as a seed grows into a plant, the individual develops into a full differentiated, balanced, and unified personality. That, at least, is the direction development takes, although the goal of complete differentiation, balance, and unity is rarely if ever reached, except, as Jung observes, by a Jesus or a Buddha. This striving for self-realization or consummate selfhood is archetypal, that is to say, inborn. No one can avoid the powerful influence of this unity archetype, although what course its expression may take and how successful one may be in realizing the aim varies from person to person.[51]

Specifically regarding archetypes, not only does each system become differentiated from the other systems, as when ego differentiates from the shadow, but also each system differentiates within its own structure and becomes more and more complex. For instance, archetypes as well as unconscious personal complexes "express themselves in more subtle and intricate ways as they become individualized."[52] This is why children's pastimes and simplistic stories are not satisfying to adults, who need far more complex symbolic systems, as found for instance in the arts, religion, and dreams.

Because society, especially our contemporary world, does not adequately allow for, as an example, the shadow's expressions of its primitive, instinctual needs, they are unhealthily repressed. Thus, it [the shadow] returns to the unconscious sphere of personality, where it remains in a primitive, undifferentiated state. Then when it breaks through the barrier of repression—as it is bound to do from time to time—the shadow manifests itself in sinister, pathological ways. The savage sadism of modern warfare and the crude obscenities of pornography exemplify the actions of an undifferentiated shadow.[53]

Consequently, it is important that all archetypes become conscious and recognized as functioning elements of a healthy personality. It is my opinion that, through dreams, archetypes find needed expression, for dreams bring to consciousness that which is unconscious. In fact, the process of awakening to wisdom—what can be perceived as the education of an individual—finds its root in the Latin *educatio* (bringing up, drawing out, or raising) and *educo* (I raise up). "Education, as the etymology of the word indicates, is a drawing out from the person of something that is already there in a nascent state, and not the filling up of an empty container with knowledge."[54]

Jung often used his dreams[55] and the dreams and creative visions of patients to explore the process of individuation, through which analysands could translate unconscious dream elements via diverse creative genres. Eliminating conscious control over the psychic imagery is the key to understanding what Jung termed "Active Imagination." At eighty-one years of age, Jung undertook the recordings of his life story; in the completed project entitled *Memories, Dreams, Reflections*,[56] he discussed the process of how dream interpretation can lead to individuation and mental health. As Jung explains, through the application of Active Imagination techniques, dreams become "bridges" that connect the conscious ego, the "I," with the collective unconscious.

Jung also likened the process of Active Imagination to that of alchemy in the sense that both deal with and seek to achieve a morphological "oneness." As Jung explains, humans begin in a unified state, a single cell "at one" with all life, that constantly undergoes a continuous process of differentiation and alienation from the "all else." Active Imagination in dreams seeks to "weave" all of the separate pieces back into one collective whole by allowing dream images, moods, and body sensations to take concrete form by reproducing them through diverse modes of creative media: painting, dance, music, sculpture, writing, etc. Giving free rein to one's unbridled imagination through a multitude of different means of expression awakens the "transcendent function" that unites opposites and reunifies them to recreate the original undifferentiated healthy state.

In this sense, Active Imagination is similar to the Freudian concept of "free association," but it uses various creative modes of expression to draw emotions as symbols, then interprets metaphors through three perspectives: personal, collective, and archetypal. As an example, a kiss may be (as the familiar song from *Casablanca* informs) "still a kiss"; however, simultaneously it is so much more. On a personal level, it could symbolize very pleasurable emotions, but it could also conjure disturbing associations as well, especially if the kiss were not welcomed. Similarly, viewed from a collective perspective, a kiss has many possible connotations. For many Mediterranean and European cultures, it is a warm greeting, usually on the cheeks—given openly even to strangers. On a very different, perhaps somewhat unexpected level, to organized crime figures, it is a symbol of impending destruction in response to betrayal, as in "the kiss of death." To many other cultures, kissing can be an extremely private expression of affection, one not to be practiced in public. And lastly, on an archetypal level, it can be viewed as a symbolic expression of the universal concept of the coming together of opposites in one complementary figure, for instance in the *Taoist* yin/yang iconic imagery.

By drawing, narrating, acting out, dancing, etc. dream imagery, patients not only communicate freely the content of the unconscious but also recognize changes that may occur when consciousness interferes with the process of communications from the psyche. Providing a technique to allow dream elements to "act themselves out" helps make them visible, thereby creating a better understanding of one's self and, more importantly, awakening the individual to identification with the archetypes of the collective unconscious. Jung explains the importance of active imagination as conduit to unconscious "fantasies,"

> Another source for the material we need is to be found in "active imagination." By this I mean a sequence of fantasies produced by deliberate concentration… From this I have drawn the conclusion that dreams often contain fantasies which "want" to become conscious. The sources of dreams are often repressed instincts which have a natural tendency to influence the conscious mind. In cases of this sort, the patient is simply given the task of contemplating any one fragment of fantasy

that seems significant to him—a chance idea, perhaps, or something he has become conscious of in a dream—until its context becomes visible, that is to say, the relevant associative material in which it is embedded.[57]

Before embarking on a brief exploration of some central archetypes, it is important to note here that the process of active imagination does have its dangers. By identifying too strongly and readily with elements of the collective unconscious, individuals could be drawn away from the reality of everyday waking life, so such a process should be selectively applied. In regards to the potential risk, Jung admonishes: "Suffice it to say that the resultant sequence of fantasies relieves the unconscious and produces material rich in archetypal images and associations. Obviously, this is a method that can only be used in certain carefully selected cases. The method is not entirely without danger, because it may carry the patient too far away from reality. A warning against thoughtless application is therefore in place."[58] Nevertheless, proper and professional utilization of active imagination can awaken individuals to the process of individuation, through which not only the dissociated elements of the psyche could be individually recognized and made whole, but also the self could achieve integration and unification.

As can be imagined, the amount of archetypes could approach infinite levels; however, Jung particularly recognized the powerful influences of the shadow and anima/animus, which will be the focus of this study preceded by a brief discussion of the persona.

Persona

The persona is often identified as a "mask"[59] which the ego wears; however, psychoanalytically this is not quite accurate. Rather, "the persona is simply a structure for relating to the collective conscious situation, analogous to the concept of role in social theory."[60] As such, in dreams as in waking life, it is often portrayed by objects such as clothing, which can be put on or taken off. Its role is to facilitate the ego's ability to interact healthily with its societal environment. It can also be a vehicle for transformation, through which the ego can change and adapt. Consequently, to positively affect mental health, when the persona is encountered in dreams, it must be analyzed in terms of its relationship with all elements of the dream landscape.

Shadow

Similarly, the shadow can also be misunderstood and all too often is. It is commonly and erroneously perceived to be an evil or negative force; however, it more specifically relates to some dissociation (usually occurring in early childhood) of the ego from normal societal behavior. For example, a child can or be made to conform to her or his family life even though that family may be quite dysfunctional. When this child matures, his or her dysfunctional "shadow" must be recognized and revised to refashion a healthier ego, so the child can live and survive in society. If this is not accomplished, the ego will, in most cases, project the shadow onto others, especially other members of the same sex, and create irrational barriers to impede communication or interaction with these members of society, where it may appear as its opposite—for example, a passive ego will present itself as being in aggressive danger— or it may appear as an exaggerated version of itself, more passive than in waking consciousness. Healing can result from reintegrating the shadow with more normal societal paradigms. Consequently, one of the functions of dreams may be to illuminate the shadow archetype as a first step towards such recognition. In dreams, "the shadow may contain qualities that need to be integrated for a more comprehensive ego structure."[61] Admittedly, however, simply recognizing these qualities does not always allow for their application to be easily applied to one's waking life:

> The shadow is a moral problem that challenges the whole ego personality, for no one can become conscious of the shadow without considerable moral effort. To become conscious of it involves recognizing the dark aspects of the personality as present and real. This act is the essential condition for any kind

of self-knowledge, and it therefore, as a rule, meets with considerable resistance. Indeed, self-knowledge as a psychotherapeutic measure frequently requires much painstaking work extending over a long period.[62]

Further complicating the realignment of the shadow is its emotional identity, which is not a product of one's conscious manufacture; rather, it emanates from uncontrollable unconscious forces. "Emotion, incidentally, is not an activity of the individual but something that happens to him."[63] Thus, the shadow is, in good part, formed early-on from the interactions of the ego with society; hence, its nature can be recognized in dreams from the material of the personal unconscious as a reactionary formation. Therefore, restoring mental health depends upon the reabsorption of projections created during early childhood. Consequently, identifying these projections in dreams is a positive first step to an individual's ability to rejoin society in a healthy manner.

Anima/Animus

"The anima or animus primarily serves the function of enlarging the personal sphere, which includes the inner 'space' of ego, persona and shadow as well as that of the anima and animus."[64] It is of some value here to review Jung's concept of the ego. As Hall and Nordby explain:

> The ego is the name Jung uses for the organization of the conscious mind; it is composed of conscious perceptions, memories, thoughts, and feelings. Although the ego occupies a small portion of the total psyche, it plays the vitally important function of gatekeeper to consciousness. Unless the ego acknowledges the presence of an idea, a feeling, a memory, a perception, it cannot be brought into awareness. The ego is highly selective. It resembles a distillery; much psychic material is fed into it but little comes out or reaches the level of full awareness. Every day we are subjected to a vast number of experiences, most of which do not become conscious because the ego eliminates them before they reach consciousness. This is an

important function, for otherwise we would be overwhelmed by the mass of material that would crowd into consciousness.[65]

Through this process, the ego allows for a continuity of personality and creates the sense that we are this day essentially who we were in previous days. This has, in turn, a conscious influence on one's ability to become differentiated. Simply put, the more individualized a person may become, the more intensely experienced unconscious archetypal elements can be brought to consciousness.[66]

In dreams, the "enlarging" of the personal sphere is often accomplished by projecting the anima (affinity with male inner femininity) or animus (affinity with female inner masculinity) onto either an opposite sex figure or onto characters in myths and fairytales. Jung defines the anima/animus as "the projection-making factor,"[67] which when it occurs in dreams, for instance, "takes on personified form" and "embodies all the outstanding characteristics" of a masculine or feminine being.[68]

Speaking in generalities for the purpose of this study, males tend to project the anima onto the women in their lives, who then assume the burden of carrying out what males may perceive to be "women's work." An example would be a husband leaving all the writing of "thank you" notes and all of the holiday shopping for the family to his wife instead of doing it himself. Conversely, females will often internalize the animus, projecting it inward, where it becomes a critical voice constantly questioning their strengths, abilities, and appearance. An illustration of this introspection would be; a woman walking into a room filled with strangers and wondering how these "others" perceive her.

Using the analogy of a "bag" to stand for the repressed contents of one's unconscious, Robert Bly differentiates the way men and women suppress or put into the bag the anima and animus respectively, only to subsequently project them onto others, and the resulting dangerously unhealthy mental consequences:

I think we could say that most males in our culture put their feminine side or interior woman into the bag. When they begin, perhaps around thirty-five or forty, trying to get in touch with the feminine side again, she may be by then truly hostile to them. The same man may experience in the meantime much hostility from women in the outer world. The rule seems to be: the outside has to be like the inside. That's the way it is on this globe. If a woman, wanting to be approved for her femininity, has put her masculine side or her internal male into the bag, she may find that twenty years later he will be hostile to her. Moreover, he may be unfeeling and brutal in his criticism. She's in a spot. Finding a hostile man to live with would give her someone to blame, and take away the pressure, but that wouldn't help the problem of the closed bag. In the meantime, she is liable to sense a double rejection, from the male inside and the male outside. There's a lot of grief in this whole thing.[69]

Through dream analysis, analysands can better achieve individualization by learning how to withdraw these projections to increase the scope of their personal consciousness, thereby creating more realistic relationships with members of the opposite sex. If not, one's projections onto self or the other can become terribly disappointing and quite painful when one realizes that the manufactured projections are mere fantasy: " Failure to withdraw a projection onto, for example, a loved one, may lead to an embittered and shallow relationship—the former loved one does not live up to expectations, he or she is found to be not the person the projection promised."[70]

James Hall illustrates how dream interpretation can bring to light the process of anima/animus projection through this *denouement* of one of his patient's dreams:

…[The] woman dreamed that she was fishing in a boat with her father when something was caught on the line. Although it was her line, her father reeled in the fish, seeming to use all his strength. For some time she resisted the thought that she was relying too much on the figure of the father as animus, focusing rather on the interpretation that the dream showed her father "finally" doing something for her. She was an exceptionally intelligent and creative woman who doubted unnecessarily her own abilities—that is, the abilities were present but unconscious (in the animus), not integrated into the tacit functional structure of the ego.[71]

Having the ability to withdraw her animus projection from her father would allow this woman to recognize her talents and awaken her to the fact that she, herself, is the source of the strength she visualizes in her dream; this would result in the creation of a healthier personality through the enlargement of her individualized self. Therefore, by recognizing their anima/animus projections in dreams and withdrawing them, analysands can form genuine relationships rather than idealized imitations, which are doomed to failure when the reality of the partner is contrasted to the idealized projection.

Thus, when dreams are recognized as diagnostic tools, they become powerful vehicles to the effecting of mental health. In Jungian terms, true mental health is achieved via an individualization process of "wholeness," which he asserts to be:

...[I]n effect, the spontaneous realization of the whole man. The ego-conscious personality is only a part of the whole man, and its life does not yet represent his total life. The more he is merely "I," the more he splits himself off from the collective man, of whom he is also a part, and may even find himself in opposition to him. But since everything living strives for wholeness, the inevitable one-sidedness of our conscious life is continually being corrected and compensated by the universal human being in us, whose goal is the ultimate integration of conscious and unconscious, or better, the assimilation of the ego to a wider personality.[72]

Through dreams, all four aspects of the personal and collective human being can be recognized and, thereby, rejoined to create an undifferentiated, healthy "whole" person, an individualized self.

Gestalt: Frederick "Fritz" Perls

Once a Freudian analyst, later a major exponent of gestalt therapy, Frederick "Fritz" Perls believed that dreams project missing, or disowned, portions of the self. In essence, we possess emotional "holes," so mental health can be affected through a process of refilling the gaps that dreams uncover to recreate the wholeness of a unified individual. However, these missing elements of the psyche can only be recognized by viewing the entirety of the "field" (fore and ground) rather than through analysis of its pieces. In order to do so, this perception eschews interpretation by "expert" analysts in favor of an individualistic approach, whereby the dreamer comes to an epiphany by participating solely in the moment and addressing any metaphorical dream elements on an individual, role-playing basis rather than through the adoption of universal symbolism. This methodology requires a great deal of devotion, time and hard work. As Perls explains: "In therapy, we have not only to get through the role-playing. We also have to fill in the holes in the personality to make the person whole and complete again. And again, as before, this can't be done by turner-ons. In Gestalt Therapy we have a better way, but it is no magic short-cut. You don't have to be on a couch or in a Zendo[73] for twenty or thirty years, but you have to invest yourself, and it takes time to grow."[74]

From the German, gestalt means "shape" or "form"; hence, it does not break down the dream to analyze individual elements; instead, it focuses on the entire form, as if it were occurring in the present moment and not as some remembrance of a fractured substitute reality: "Gestalt therapy theory applies holism at several levels of its structure, and gestalt therapy practice views that practice as one whole process. The theory of gestalt therapy is both a property and a nomological holism; that is, its characteristics can only be understood in context of the whole approach, and its principles work together. The practice of gestalt therapy is a methodological holism, given that the laws of each part of gestalt therapy are shaped by all the laws of all the parts working together rather than any set of laws alone."[75]

Consequently, it is necessary to acknowledge what one is feeling and behaving in the "here and now." Because Perls believed that we instinctively know our biological needs, which he termed "end-goals," he posited that mental health problems arise when we suppress or replace end-goals with sublimations and, thereby, lose sight of them. However, if both the figure (end-goal) and its ground (the poorly defined background) are not recognized, they overwhelm consciousness; therefore, to affect mental health, one must comprehend the wholeness of the "field," that is the juxtaposition of figure and ground.[76] Any disruption of the field is a "growth disorder." The aim of Gestalt therapy is to reverse this stunting of the growth process in order to effect positive mental health. Thus, one must be aware of, and in contact with, the wholeness of the field.

Gestalt-based therapy's holistic approach avers that the whole is more/greater than the sum of its parts. The tendency for growth to include an emergent quality of contact and relationships precludes a reductionist perspective of the element of healing. Gestalt therapy is ready to articulate these changes in approach from heroic utilitarianism to reverent hospitality. This involves a withdrawal of projections and a shift from telling to listening.[77]

To achieve this goal, one must be self-regulating, not dependent on others. Therefore, gestalt dream analysis requires a great deal of self-reflection and acting out. Only by literally performing a dream, wherein one assumes the role of every actor and element of it, can one get a sense of the totality of its meaning. This performance exercise is termed the "empty chair" technique. During a Gestalt Therapy workshop at the Esalen Institute (1968), Perls set-up a role-playing session with these instructions:

Now, I want you all to talk to your dreams, and let the dreams talk back—not the content, but as if the dreams were a thing. "Dreams, you are frightening me," "I don't want to know about you," or something, and let the dreams answer back. So, now, I would like each one of you to play the role of their dreams, such as, "I only seldom come to you, and then only in little bits and pieces," or however you experience your dreams. I want you to *be* that dream. Reverse the role, so that you are the dream, and talk to the whole group, as if you were the dream talking to yourself.[78]

To illustrate the process here, during one of my public lectures at an assisted living facility, a senior citizen (well into his eighties) openly shared his dream with the audience. First, he provided some brief background material: He is a widower with one adult married daughter. He has two grandchildren. He likes his independence and is proud of the fact that he has enough money saved to afford living in a fairly affluent adult facility. He stated that he was "well off" but certainly not wealthy. He related the following dream: He saw himself on an operating table. There were two doctors—one male, one female—both obviously strangers, yet he still felt that he recognized them and knew who they were. However, because they were wearing surgical masks, identifying them was all the more difficult. He stated in no uncertain terms that he knew the surgery was unnecessary and painful, and most importantly, that he didn't want or need it. He felt that he would be losing something important. But he felt trapped, that he could not escape because they were tireless in their insistence and used every means of persuasion to convince him that he should let them continue with their operation.

We set up some chairs in a semi-circle, and he labelled them in accordance with the characters in his dream: himself, the male surgeon, and the female surgeon. He immediately elected to sit in the chair labelled "female surgeon," and almost as soon as he sat, he knew what his dream meant. As he explained, the two surgeons were his daughter and her husband (his son-in-law), but they had changed so much that he hardly recognized them (hence the masks). Instead of the supportive children he needed and knew, they became "operators," in that they were relentlessly "operating on him" to fund a business venture that they wished to start. Every time he saw them, they would try to get the money from him, even to the point of using his love of his grandchildren as sources of guilt, but each time he would refuse because he felt that the savings he had managed "to squirrel away" were essential to maintaining not only his independence but also his care.

As a result, through the empty chair technique, this gentleman gained the awareness of who he is and what he wants in the moment, and it gave him the strength to stand up for himself. To emphasize this belief in the need for each of us to become real and to understand that in the "here and now," in this moment, one cannot possibly be any different from who one is, Frederick "Fritz" Perls gave us this Gestalt prayer:

> I do my thing, and you do your thing.
> I am not in this world to live up to your expectations
> And you are not in this world to live up to mine.
> You are you and I am I,
> And if by chance we find each other, it's beautiful.
> If not, it can't be helped.[79]

Phenomenology: Medard Boss

Medard Boss was analyzed by Freud and studied with Jung, but as with many of the early proponents of psychoanalysis, he rebelled against traditional theories and developed the *daseinsanalytic*[80] approach in opposition to the classical intrapsychic modalities. Boss strongly believed dreaming to be similar to the waking state in that both are responses to the meaningful existence of phenomena in the world, hence the term "phenomenology." Boss explained that there are two basic steps to understanding his theory:

> We must first consider exactly for what phenomena the
> dreamer's existence is so open that they may have entered and
> shone forth into its understanding light. This in turn tells us

what phenomena are not accessible to the perception of his dreaming state…the dreamer's existence is still closed. As a second step, we need to determine *how* the dreamer conducts himself toward whatever is revealed to him in the clearance of his dreaming world, particularly the mood that predicates this way of behaving. If both of these can be accurately described, we reached a full understanding of the dreamer's existence during the dream period.[81]

Succinctly, step one would be to determine exactly what phenomena in the waking world are finding expression, or are being revealed, during the dreaming state. The second step would be to then recognize how the dreamer responds to these revelations of the phenomena intruding into his or her dreams. What is the dreamer's mood and, more importantly, what is happening in waking life to predicate such emotional reactions? Thus, to Boss, dreams are always anchored in, or need to be bridged to, the present.

However, dreams are not as clear as waking states because they are dim reflections of our stronger rational abilities to comprehend waking experiences. Although both states, waking and dreaming, are processing one's experiences with phenomena, as Boss sees it, while awake we are far more "clear-sighted" than while dreaming. As a result, Boss does not advance any classical psychoanalytic conception of the existence of an unconscious; therefore, dreams do not present any occult workings of some unintelligible unconscious state. Rather, they are analogous to waking states. In essence, dreams are efforts to understand conscious phenomena and not messages from some source of personal or collective unconscious wisdom. To simplify, while awake we use the strength of our reasoning powers but while asleep, we use our emotions to understand and interact with the phenomena of this world.

Therefore, despite the limited reasoning abilities of dream consciousness, dreams are valuable because they can effectively generate and communicate *emotive* reactions to waking phenomena which, when added to the process of conscious reasoning, can be valuable insights to the mood of an analysand to reveal how s/he is dealing with the waking issues of her/his life:

> The very peculiarity of the dreaming state… that is, its limited existential range relative to the waking state, lends dreaming its great importance for therapy. While it may be said that dreaming existence is less open than its waking counterpart, often enough a person is exposed to unfamiliar significances *for the first time ever* while dreaming. Of course, significances that have never yet been countenanced in waking life tend to appear in dreaming, as every meaning does, only from alien sensory presences of entities. Yet there is some advantage in the fact that in those massive, materially visible forms, significances do not merely suggest themselves but strike the dreamer forcibly.[82]

To Boss, the value of dream interpretation lies in the dreamer's ability to emotively "feel" the consequences of phenomena in contrast to waking state rationalizations of one's emotions, which tend to mask one's mood and, thereby, impede an understanding of just how powerful the effect of said phenomena may be on an individual. Just as one has two eyes—one being dominant—with each providing its own perspective, one perceives the phenomena of one's existence predominantly through the waking eye augmented by the emotive inner vision of dreaming consciousness.

Boss' phenomenological approach to dream interpretation challenges both Freud and Jung. For example, Freud and Jung desired to know, as thoroughly as possible, an analysand's personal history. Freud, in particular, sought the dreamer's "free association" to provide clues to the workings of his patients' unconscious and as importantly, pursued hints to repressed issues being disguised to avoid censorship but still being communicated through dream imagery. Conversely, Boss believed that both free association as well as the patient's personal history were unimportant and should, therefore, be purged from the interpretation process.

Boss also disagreed with Jung. Jung did not share Freud's interest in free associations, as he was curious about examining every part of the dream as elements of a "whole" dramatic structure; therefore, he focused on images that symbolically recreated and/or related emotive states and did not stray from the text of any specific dream. In contrast, Boss disregarded metaphorical analyses in favor of relating dream elements to materials drawn exclusively from the actual experiences of a dreamer's waking state. He especially argued against archetypal interpretation:

> ...[J]ung, in his atomization of the "system of psychic balance," arrived at the :archetypes" as the element or sources of energy of the latter, and at the idea of the "collective unconscious" as the assembly of all the "archetypes."

> However, an archetype deduced from the mere identity of events, i.e. from something logically universal, is no more than a mentally derived hypothesis having an extremely small probability of actual existence. Jung himself therefore has to admit that no one will ever know if there are archetypes at all, when he allows his pupil Jacobi to say that one can never meet an archetype directly.[83]

Consequently, Boss would ask analysands to "bridge" dream situations to waking phenomena. What is happening in the dreamer's waking state that could precipitate the dream situation and create its imagery? Boss believed that, once these dreaming situations could be tied to waking phenomena, the waking consciousness of an analysand could then process the dream information and realize a course of action. Because the dream state is limited in its perceptual abilities, its materials must be linked to waking situations in order to be understood and to assist in the healing process of an analysand's disturbed mental condition.

To Boss, the goal of analysis is "illumination"; therefore, any resistance is perceived to be a defense mechanism, which ironically sentences one to live in darkness. Darkness is the "blocking of light," not a force itself. Thus, the obstruction must be removed; one must deal with experiences, fears, attitudes, and beliefs that are hindering the natural flow of light from the "core self." *Dasein* is the fundamental core that illuminates us and generates healing and wellbeing. Simply as a means of trying to understand, I envision the Jain idea of the soul as a clear prism, one that gets tarnished with experience; thus, enlightenment is achieved through the cleansing of it in order to liberate its light. Similarly, in *The Gospel of Judas,* a gnostic text, Judas is portrayed as "heroic," for it is he who releases Jesus from the imprisonment of his mortal body to allow him to return to the "light."

Judas finally betrays Jesus in the *Gospel of Judas*, but he does so knowingly, and at the sincere request of Jesus. Jesus says to Judas, with reference to the other disciples, "You will exceed all of them. For you will sacrifice the man that clothes me." According to the *Gospel of Judas*, Jesus is a savior not because of the mortal flesh that he wears but because he can reveal the soul or spiritual person who is within, and the true home of Jesus is not this imperfect world below but the divine world of light and life.[84]

Please note here an important caveat: The analogies presented above are only meant to provide a simple means of envisioning the illuminating core. Therefore, it is not my intention to suggest in any way that there is a spiritual element in Boss' theory of the illuminating core itself; rather, the truth is exactly the opposite: Boss' concept is one based totally in the phenomenological realm of experiential knowledge and one's enlightenment about how one interacts with its realities.

However, the analogies do suggest flaws in a theory that rejects all but conscious origins of a core self. Boss' theory does have its detractors. His disbelief in, and limiting of, the existence of an unconscious origin of dreams can be countered by the opposing recognition of the unconscious as a vital source of dream wisdom unavailable to waking consciousness, which actually is itself negatively limited by sensory input and/or experiential events. Additionally, Boss does not mention the use of incubation, or any other means of directing dreaming. He has little to say about what qualities are inherently feminine or masculine. Given his commitment not to engage in unprovable speculation, he does not define the male and female psyches, nor any architecture of psychological mechanisms in something called the psyche, which itself he sees as an unnecessary hypothetical construct.[85]

Children's Dreams: Anna Freud and Melanie Klein

Anna Freud

Recognized as the founder of child psychoanalysis, Anna Freud was not only a major proponent of her father's theories, but also she was a pathfinder in her own right. Specifically, in fact, she differed from Sigmund Freud on the issue of child psychoanalysis. Whereas her father insisted that the unconscious is the origin of personality construction, Anna believed that developmental stages are the source of personality formulation in children. Thus, she emphasized the significance of the ego, especially in the formation of defense mechanisms, a theory which refutes Sigmund Freud's fervent insistence on the importance of the id. To Anna, dreams help bring to light the functioning of both the id and the ego: "Dream interpretation, then, assists us in our investigation of the id, insofar as it is successful in bringing to light latent dream thoughts (id content), and in our investigation of the ego institutions and their defensive operations, insofar as it enables us to reconstruct the measures adopted by the censor from their effect upon the dream thoughts."[86]

Contemporary research appears to support Anna Freud's assumption about the impact of developmental stages on children's dreams. A special issue of *Dreaming: Journal of the Association for the Study of Dreams* focused on emerging trends in the field of children's dreams and nightmares. One common thread that ran throughout the diverse range of articles was the finding that the difficulties of ego maturation through developmental stages, especially in the transition from adolescence to teenage years, were the most prevalent theme in children's dreams: "Moving from childhood toward young adulthood, the increased mixture of active participation in dreams parallels the flowering of ego strength, cognitive powers, physical capacities, and independent functioning in the world. Children are dependent and have less mastery of their world and less ability to defend themselves against the waking emotional and physical survival challenges. Their dreams reflect their limited capacity for assertion and independence. By young adulthood, maturation of independent functioning is reflected in dream content."[87]

Perhaps it can be said that Anna's own defenses against the traumas and anxieties of her childhood may have been the stimuli for studying psychoanalysis (as a means of identification with her father) and for her focus on the analysis of children (as a means of resolving her own ego issues, especially sibling rivalry). Anna did not have a good relationship with her mother or her siblings and was especially envious of her older sister Sophie, who was praised as the "beauty" of the family. In fact, Anna underwent analysis with her father, with whom she identified, and for whom she later became principal caretaker. This and her experience working with children at wartime nurseries[88] may be the impetus of her work and bases of her theories.

Specifically regarding dreams, Anna Freud realized that the techniques of classical analysis, especially its "mainstay" free association, could not be successfully employed with children. Consequently, the child-analyst must interpret the connections of "the manifest dream content and the latent dream thoughts according to his own intimate knowledge of the child's inner situation at the time of dreaming."[89] Nevertheless, she alleged that whatever success an analyst could have with adult dreams could be similarly achieved with children's dreams. As she explains:

> The child dreams neither more nor less than the adult in analysis; as in everyone, the clarity or incomprehensibility of the dream contents depends upon the strength of the resistance. The dreams of children are certainly easier to interpret, even if in the analysis they are not always as simple as the examples given in *"The Interpretation of Dreams"* [sic] (Freud). We find in them all the distortions of wish fulfillment corresponding to the complicated neurotic organization of the child patient. But nothing is easier for the child to comprehend than the interpretation of dreams.[90]

She also believed that children truly enjoyed the "game" of dream interpretation:

> The child amuses himself with the search for individual dream elements as with a Chinese puzzle, following with much satisfaction the individual images or words into the situations of actual life. Perhaps this occurs because the child is nearer to dreams than the adult; perhaps it is only on this account that he is not astonished to find a meaning in the dream because he has never heard the scientific view that dreams are only nonsense. In any case the child is proud of a successful dream interpretation.[91]

Her enthusiasm about the use of dreams as an effective component of child analysis motivated her to state boldly that even the most unintelligent children, otherwise difficult to analyze, could be reached through interpreting their dreams. One reason for this success results from the limited day experiences of children, whose activities are less complicated and more centrally located than adults. Similarly, as a rule, children experience far less contact with a variety of individuals in sophisticated interactions than do adults.

Of course, being a traditional Freudian analyst, Anna could not help but to interpret children's dreams as they related to sexual developmental stages. For example, she describes the dream of a nine year old girl who dreaded lighting the gas-heater for fear of an explosion; as a result, she suffered much anxiety and had disturbing dreams. In one such dream, she could not find anyone to light the heater, as her mother was absent, and her nurse and brother could not do it. This dream was repeated during the next night but in a slightly different way: This time, she attempted to light the gas-heater but could not, so it exploded. As punishment, the nurse held her in the fire to burn up. The girl believed the second dream was about punishment. Anna Freud agreed but further interpreted both dreams in terms of the girl's anxiety and guilt over masturbation:

> She could give no further associations, which in this case, however, I could easily supply. Obviously playing with the stove stood for playing with her own body, which she also assumed in the case of her brother. The "wrongness" about it was the expression of her own criticism; the explosion probably the form of her orgasm. As a consequence, the nurse, who represents the admonisher against masturbation, carries out the punishment.[92]

Although Anna Freud stressed the importance of dream interpretation in child analyses, she also utilized other methodologies (as did Melanie Klein), for example the drawings of children and the interpretation of their daydreams. In essence, daydreams are "mini" self-hypnotic episodes, in which the child enters a hypnogogic condition, wherein one is straddling the mystical limen between dream and waking states. Anna praises the use of daydreams in the analysis of children because, "They discuss them more readily and are obviously less ashamed than the adult, who condemns his fancies as childish."[93]

Yet despite the similarities of their psychoanalytic approach to child analysis, Anna had differences with her colleague and fellow child psychoanalytic pioneer, Melanie Klein.

Melanie Klein

One of the best yet relatively unsung analysts, Melanie Klein, also pioneered the field of child psychoanalysis. Recognizing the difficulty in collecting data from children through the traditional methodology of verbal "free" associations, Klein believed that it was important to create alternative venues for children to spark their imaginations: "…[I]t is above all important with children to set their phantasy free and to induce them to phantasy."[94] One of these ways is through the interpretation of their dreams. To Klein, however, dreams are just one of the ways that children express themselves; therefore, allowing them to draw, to relate day-dreams and, most importantly, to "play" are all processes that can be used to analyze children because when children play actively, they are communicating symbolically. This symbolic nature of play and dreams becomes Klein's key to analyzing children.

Freud has taught us to approach the language of dreams. Symbolism is only a part of it. If we wish to understand the child's play correctly in relation to its whole behavior during the analytic session we must not be content to pick out the meaning of the separate symbols in the play, striking as they often are, but must take into consideration all the mechanisms and methods of representation employed by the dream-work, never losing sight of the relation of each factor to the situation as a whole. Early analysis of children has shown again and again how many different meanings a single toy or a single bit of play can have, and that we can only infer and interpret their meaning when we consider their wide connections and the whole analytic situation in which they are set.[95]

Nevertheless, Klein does state that all of these creative exercises, including dream interpretation, are analytical when they are understood as symbolic manifestations of the child's unconscious: " For this is just the lever which we must make use of in child-analysis. A child will bring us an abundance of phantasies if we follow him along this path with the conviction that what he recounts is symbolic."[96]

In this, she opposes Anna Freud's belief that dream interpretation is the "royal road" to child analysis and counters Anna's doubts about Klein's utilization of observed symbolic communications for analytical purposes. Anna Freud argued against the "play technique," believing it to be merely an observational, behavioral tool, rather than a psychoanalytic methodology. Klein refuted that criticism:

> She [Anna Freud] thinks it doubtful whether one is justified in interpreting the content of the drama enacted in children's play as symbolic and thinks that they might very likely be occasioned simply by actual observations or experiences of daily life. Here I must say that from Anna Freud's illustrations of my technique, I can see that she misunderstands it. "If the child overturns a lamp-post or a toy figure she interprets it as something of an aggressive impulse against the father; a deliberate collision between two cars as evidence of an observation of sexual union between the parents' (p. 29) [of Anna Freud's *The Psychoanalytical Treatment of Children*]. I should never attempt any such "wild" symbolic interpretations of children's play.[97]

Klein defends her technique by equating her psychoanalytical treatment of children at play to the same process Sigmund Freud used in the analysis of adults. To Klein, Freud's dream-work methodologies apply to the play of children, as well as to their dreams. Consequently, she perceives her play technique to be the child's equivalent to an adult's forming of a psychoanalytic transference. As such, children's play, like the dreams of adults, provides little ones with a means of "living out and working through that original situation in phantasy." Once the origin of the child's traumas can be recognized, corrective measures can be applied to effect mental healing and reestablish proper developmental growth patterns.[98] Klein concludes:

> Supposing that a child gives expression to the same psychic material in various repetitions—often actually through various media, *i.e.* toys, water, by cutting-out, drawing, etc.—and supposing that, besides, I can observe that these particular activities are mostly accompanied at the time by a sense of guilt, manifesting itself either as anxiety or in representations which imply over-compensation, which are the expression of reaction-formations—supposing, then, that I have arrived at an insight into certain connections: then I interpret these phenomena and link them up with the Ucs [unconscious] and the analytic situation. The practical and theoretical conditions for the interpretation are precisely the same as in the analysis of adults.[99]

Group/*Psi* Dreams: Montague Ullman

Trained as a psychiatrist and psychoanalyst, Montague Ullman was one of the major dream analysts of the late twentieth century. He founded the Maimonides Dream Laboratory and championed the "group" approach to dream analysis. Like Perls, Ullman sought to shift the interpretation of dreams from the hands of experts to the dreamers themselves. He believed that a group approach eliminated the need for a controlling analyst; each member of the group was an equal participant and had an equal voice. The dreamer shared her/his dream and was helped by the group to reconnect with the original emotions s/he experienced during the dream. In further resistance to Freud, Ullman believed that free association was not enough. Dreamers also needed group feedback, in the form of questions, to draw out repressed materials.[100] As a result, dreams themselves, with the assistance of trusted group members rather than an analyst, become healing devices:

Working with dreams in a small group setting has enriched and, in some ways, modified the view I had of dreams as a practicing psychoanalyst. For one thing, it has brought me closer to seeing the dream in its self-healing potential. It is available as an instrument by means of which a greater state of wholeness can obtain. Emerging as the product of a "larger self," it confronts the dreamer with an aspect of the self that has not heretofore been acknowledged or utilized. The dream does not yield its secret easily. Work has to be done in the waking state before this healing potential can be realized.[101]

In dreams, we suspend the roles society imposes upon us. We let down the defenses we construct to protect ourselves from the truths we do not want known, not even to ourselves. To effect mental healing, dreams strip away our masks, our personae, and thrust us into a state of emotional nudity.

In addition to, and elaborating upon, his belief that "group" participation could draw a dreamer out of his/her individual psyche to join a "shared" unconsciousness, Ullman was also one of the modern-age proponents of *psi* dreaming: the connection of that which pertains to psychic and parapsychological phenomena in dreams. However, as he admits, although the experience of these types of dreams is commonplace, scientific evidence of *psi* powers in humans is not easily proven: "Like many others I have had, on occasion, dreams that struck me as paranormal. Experiences of this kind deepened my belief in the reality of psychic phenomena, but did little in the way of advancing its scientific standing."[102]

Nevertheless, despite the difficulty of providing scientific certainty, Ullman was one of the champions of Vigilance Theory's relevance to paranormal dreaming. Briefly, on a psychological level, Vigilance Theory links the metaphoric character of dreams to an intrapersonal awakening that connects the individual dreamer to her or his identification with all humanity.

Such experiences may indicate that psi is extraordinarily more complex than commonly realized, since there is no easy classification of psi events into "cause" and "effect." One might speculate that human relationships may be guided and influenced by some fundamental underlying force that occasionally surfaces into consciousness as psi events, particularly during emotion-laden situations. Perhaps, during these times, a collective consciousness is formed between the individuals involved.[103]

A priori, metaphors structure dreams. Metaphors relate hermetic enigmas in concrete terms, for example through the use of Robert Burns' simile: "My love is like a red, red rose," whereby the abstract construct of love is communicated through the concreteness of "red, red" and "rose." Thus, the abstract emotion of love is defined via the sensory perceptions of color and natural object. But does a red, red rose really epitomize love? Of course not. There is always an element of mystery, of connection to a wisdom system beyond the dreamer's limited ability to understand. As a result, metaphors can be perceived, in a sense, to be "bridges to nowhere," in that the concrete leg of the bridge is intelligible, but the hermetic leg can never be understood. Ultimately, then, this system is intrapersonal in that it transcends one's personal knowledge base and connects (bridges) one to a structuring, universal yet incomprehensible source.

Consequently, a metaphor always finds its roots in the unknown. Therefore, a dreamer can only create these metaphors because of some connection to a hermetic source of wisdom, which the dreamer can never actually know or understand. So from where does the metaphor arise—if not from a shared, embedded, unknowable universal consciousness?

Metaphor is the initial way of grasping on to something felt and something in need of gaining expression. When a metaphor is newly created it is alive in contrast to the dead ones which have already passed into everyday speech. The live metaphor offers a creative jolt to the literalness of language. It makes use of our versatility with language, but is never quite reducible to the literalness of language. There remains something ineffably elusive about the metaphor, whether it be of the poet or of the dreamer. The same is true when we deal with a metaphor that encapsulates a psi event. We know it is true, but we know it is not true in a literal sense, and cannot be reduced to a state of literalness.[104]

To simplify, Ullman asserts, "In a tantalizing way dreams seem to originate in a source outside the self we are ordinarily familiar with while awake."[105]

Ultimately, to Ullman dreams can be recognized as figurative umbilical cords connecting the individual to the species. During waking hours, individuals face personal challenges which detach the psyche from its original universal source. As William Wordsworth admonishes in "The World is Too Much With Us":
> The world is too much with us; late and soon,
> Getting and spending, we lay waste our powers;--
> Little we see in Nature that is ours;
> We have given our hearts away, a sordid boon! (1-4)

When dreaming, the "world" disappears and waking consciousness is lulled; the personal psyche is once again miraculously awakened to its true identity as an element of a closely knit fabric of human consciousness. I am immediately reminded of a mythological metaphor of Indian origin, the "net of gems," a fabric constructed so that each intersection of netting contains a multifaceted mirror, reflecting all of the other multifaceted, reflecting mirrors. Each gem, each individual, simultaneously contains the multitude of all others while it is itself contained in, and reflected by, all the other gems. As Ullman defines it:
> Our dreaming self seems to hold onto a notion that escapes
> us in our waking moments—namely, that we are all members of
> a single species. Our historical fate has fragmented that unity,
> often in self-defeating ways, along every line of cleavage

conceivable by our ingenuity and foibles, e.g. politically, religiously, economically, ethnically, etc. This fragmenting process continues macroscopically in the way we divide the nations of the world into forces of good and evil. It goes on microscopically in the way we hurt, corrode, or destroy our sense of connection with each other, by the countless ways in which we pursue individualistic goals at the expense of others. Whereas we may be perfectly capable of living a long life as an individual thriving on dishonesty (the reverse of the adage of "the good die young"), the likelihood is that we won't long survive as a species if unchecked dishonesty undermines our humanism. And, of course, there is ample evidence currently of the danger of that possibility. The part of our being that shapes our dreams seems very much concerned with this issue. Our dreams reflect back to us with ruthless honesty how our connections to significant others fared on the previous day. We seem to have a built-in way of monitoring the extent to which inner and outer events interfere with (or enhance) our own humanity. The dream can be looked upon as a kind of steering mechanism which, if attended to, can help us stay on a survival course. Considering the calculated neglect accorded dreams on our march toward civilization it may already be too late. At any rate, it is this more global concern, one that transcends the existence of the individual as a discrete entity, that suggestively parallels or may be more intrinsically related to the way that manifestations of psi seem to have a bearing on issues of connectedness.[106]

The *psi* is the structuring pattern of dream consciousness: The *psi* nature of dreams awakens the individual to his or her connection to the "all else." In a sense, a dream is the *psychopompos,* the guide to one's soul and its "oneness" with the great mystery of life. A dream is the proverbial drop of ocean water that simultaneously contains the entire ocean within itself. As Walt Whitman sings of himself, "I am vast, I contain multitudes" (section 51). all that one can imagine, as vast as it is, is contained in one's imagination. And I am reminded too of the Native American identification with and reverence for trees and all things of nature as "thou's," in contrast to the contemporary use of the objectifying pronoun "it." To Ullman, this question of "connectedness" is the structuring pattern of dream consciousness:

> The notion of species-connectedness seems to me to be the underlying motif of our dream life. There is a part of our being that is fundamentally concerned with the survival of the species and only incidentally with the problems of the individual. The sense of our own discreteness dominates the scene while awake and we view the world and ourselves from that position. This perspective changes radically when we are asleep and dreaming. We rearrange our recent waking experience into a different order of priorities. Our dreaming self is reactive to anything in our waking experience that tampers with the state of our connectedness to others, beginning with significant persons in our life, but extending outward to all others. We reorder these experiential residues around the issue of connectedness. In our dreams we get down to basics and, from a more global perspective, see ourselves in the closely linked mosaic that makes up the human species.[107]

Lastly, Ullman believes that dreams—though they may not tell us how—keep us aware of our need to save this world, for like the fabric of the net of gems, what destroys one section destroys the entire webbing. "My point is not that dream work will save the world but that dreams can be a reminder that it needs saving."[108]

Modern Psychoanalysis: Hyman Spotnitz

"Anna O"[109] termed psychoanalysis "the talking cure." Since its earliest roots, psychoanalysis has been associated with the process of vocalizing one's thoughts and feelings. Through this process of free association, what Anna O called "chimney sweeping," an analysand can eventually achieve a transference,[110] through which she can find mental healing. Because "talking" was the vehicle through which the transference could be formulated, many believed that schizophrenic individuals could not be helped through classical psychoanalytic techniques. However, Modern Psychoanalysis is making great strides towards disproving this perception. As early as the 1930s, in fact, Medard Boss analyzed "over eight hundred dreams from schizophrenics and organic psychoses and compared them with three thousand dreams from normal individuals."[111]

Consequently, Boss was able to identify a pattern of characteristics associated with the early commencement of schizophrenia: "In the first place they are clearly distinguishable from a neurotic's dreams in that they display far more intense destructive tendencies, undisguised sexual perversions, murder, assault, and brutally thoughtless and sadistic behavior. Here it isn't so much the individual content (everybody can dream of extremely violent things) as their quantity that tips the scales."[112] Overall, he believed that he could identify three distinct types of schizophrenic patient: "Hebephrenic schizophrenia, in which he [Boss] found powerful sexual contents; catatonic schizophrenia, with aggressive impulses; and paranoid schizophrenia, with predominantly homosexual and narcissistic contents in the dreams."[113]

As can be readily imagined, there was also evidence of "splitting" behavior, whereby a schizophrenic patient divides her/his ego and objectively observes it in dreams; Boss called this "endoscopic" or self-observing: "Boss found that the ego's ability to divide itself in two and observe itself in dreams was pronounced in schizo9phrenics, and that the registering instance in the dream possessed much keener power of observation than the waking consciousness."[114] As a result, the schizophrenic dreamer can observe the destruction of himself or the world in terribly frightening detail.

In the 1950s, despite the daunting possibility of working psychoanalytically with schizophrenics, Hyman Spotnitz pioneered

"Modern Psychoanalysis," whereby the analyst attempts to bring about a "narcissistic transference" through which the analysand identifies with the analyst as if the therapist were actually a part of the patient's own mind rather than a separate individual. Spotnitz proposed that the preoedipal stage, before an individual develops language skills, is the origin of most severely ill mental patients, including schizophrenics; therefore, even schizophrenics could develop the transference necessary for effecting mental health or at least for experiencing some improvement.

In *Modern Psychoanalysis of the Schizophrenic Patient*, Spotnitz reports that there has been and continues to be successful treatment of schizophrenics through modern psychoanalytic procedures:

> Analytic psychotherapists undergoing training at centers of modern psychoanalysis have been working with schizophrenic patients since the mid-seventies. Many are postpsychotic patients beginning analytic treatment after being discharged from a psychiatric institution. The trainees do not cure all of their patients, but among them are scores of individuals previously classified as schizophrenic who are no longer schizophrenic.[115]

The obvious difficulty in treating schizophrenics psychoanalytically is their inability to communicate; however, this can be overcome by patience and avoidance of counter-transferences which arise as a result of the analyst's becoming contaminated, in a sense, by the schizophrenic's belief that he cannot be cured and, subsequently, "giving up." I witnessed the powerful effect of this counter-transference when I was training in psychoanalysis. I had the opportunity to work with a more senior analyst, who was attempting, for the first time, to analyze a schizophrenic patient who was suffering from an almost complete sense of despair and "emptiness." After my senior's session with this patient, she reported strong feelings of restlessness and that she could not stop herself from consuming an enormous amount of food, as if the patient's absolute sense of emptiness were being reenacted literally and physically in her.

Consequently, successful treatment of schizophrenics requires an analyst to first "join" the patient by sitting quietly, sometimes session after session, until the patient develops some sort of bonding necessary to form a transference.[116] Eventually, the patient feels comfortable enough to speak, even if it's just to comment on the weather. Once a conversation can occur, the analyst must avoid a negative counter-transference. At this point, the patient is essentially transferring his mental traumas onto the analyst, so the analyst can process the distressful material in a healthy manner and then send it back to the analysand, so the patient can safely reprocess it in a more beneficial manner.

Once the patient becomes responsive and has some awareness of the analyst as an "other," the patient will usually focus on five topics during a session: "current activities; past events; sex life; dreams and fantasies; and what is going on in the treatment relationship."[117] The traumas that schizophrenic patients experience occur not only during waking states but also in their dreams, and as expected, they are just as reluctant to communicate their dreams as they are to discuss their thoughts and feelings. Therefore, understanding what is "real" or merely fantasy is not an easy task, especially since schizophrenic patients perceive their painful realities and thoughts to be one and the same. As Spotnitz asserts: "Although thought, feeling, and action are the main areas in which malfunctioning is observed, it also invades the patient's fantasies and dreams. He is not disposed to report them because what he experiences in imagination is often as torturous as what he thinks and feels."[118]

As a result of the patient's silence, analysts need to be aware of "silent dream analysis," whereby the analyst, when finally presented with a patient's dream, interprets the dream himself without commenting to the patient. This "…is an essential ingredient of a successful analysis. It should go on throughout the treatment."[119]

Dreams are also important in the process of reconstruction. Even though schizophrenic patients usually have no memories of early events, they can still feel the impressions these traumas may have caused, some of which will make their appearance in dreams. Hence, dreams become another vehicle of information which can help patients reconstruct the childhood sources of trauma. By learning to recognize the patient's sources of emotional distress, an analyst can learn how to react in order to allow the patient to discharge his angst and thereby begin a process of cooperation with the analyst. "The mobilization and discharge of anger and rage free the patient to function cooperatively. When these outbursts are explored with him, he reports dreams, fantasies, or memories."[120]

Overall, dreams are one element in the treatment of schizophrenic patients, who will either overwhelm the analyst with dreams or refuse to report any; as a result, the analyst must help a patient focus on those dreams which are associated with him or her in order to collect data the patient is not consciously reporting and, thereby, may be "controlling"—possibly due to paranoia: "Early in the relationship, any dreams that are reported are studied primarily as a source of information on problems that the patient is not consciously reporting. Dreams are regarded as part of the total communication of the session, rather than as material for independent study."[121]

Revelations of unconscious psychic material are important when dealing with schizophrenics, as they are clues to preoedipal issues, but especially during the early stages of treatment, analysts must be cognizant of patient resistances to dream interpretation and practice silent analysis.

It is important that the analyst consistently interpret *to himself* dreams that are reported by the schizophrenic patient; for dreams are a major source of material on significant preoedipal experiences that the patient cannot communicate verbally. Understanding of the dreams as a form of communication aids the analyst in the process of reconstructing these events. In due time, his impressions of them will either be confirmed or corrected by further dreams. Silent analysis of the dreams may also help one decide what is causing the patient's misbehavior or how to help him give up the pathological patterns.[122]

Though dream interpretation may not be recommended for the early stages of treatment, it is an important vehicle for effecting positive change in schizophrenic patients: "The formal interpretation of dreams begins late in the treatment, when ego and object are differentiated clearly and the patient expresses a desire to understand. Although understanding for the mere purpose of satisfying his curiosity is discouraged, it is appropriate to provide understanding for the purpose of opening up avenues to more memories and more communications—a therapeutic way of facilitating change."[123]

The need to use dreams as a therapeutic way to awaken memories, create better communication skills, and thereby effect positive change is not only important for the treatment of schizophrenic patients, but also it is essential for the effecting of healthier everyday lives for everyone.

Dreams and Everyday Lives: Gayle Delaney

Gayle Delaney is the founding president of the Association for the Study of Dreams and author of numerous books on dreams. She is a talented communicator who makes the process of interpreting dreams understandable to a lay community interested in harnessing the healing potential of their dreams; for example, she even devised a dream kit organized in card-game fashion as a toolkit which any beginner can easily employ. As she asserts:

I am neither a Jungian nor a Freudian, although I owe much to these pioneers. My education as an American female of my generation has led me to question authority, and to ask questions about the usefulness of elaborate psychological theories. My theory of dream is as simple and as unassuming as I can make it.

In developing my Dream Interview Method, I have tried to keep my theoretical assumptions to a minimum.[124]

Her healthy skepticism of rigid beliefs and her inveterate curiosity are the bases of sound scholarship and allow her to question and reject what she terms "closed door" assumptions; for example, that the enigmatic language of dreams purposefully camouflages truth or that dreams are expressions of unconscious wish fulfillments. She also rebels against interpreting dreams based on one's gender, a process that is too colored by one's "biased opinions about the nature of the male and female psyches."[125] Similarly, she rejects the role of intuition for much the same reason: such an approach imposes the interpreter's personal projections rather than reveals the dreamer's associations. And though she recognizes that there are many layers of meaning in the structure of dreams, she does not believe that there can be many correct interpretations of one dream. Rather, she believes, "There may be many levels of meaning in a dream, and many ramifications of an interpretation, but they all will follow the general thrust and dramatic structure of the dream."[126]

Clearly, her focus is not on exploring the causes of dreams or on understanding why we dream; rather, she seeks to determine how insights about dreams can be positively applied to waking life. She believes that dreams metaphorically reveal our unconscious and conscious thoughts and feelings to help solve the problematic issues keeping us from living mentally healthy lives. Thus, reflecting on dream symbolism can be used to benefit dreamers and she believes that, upon waking, we have what we need to understand our dreams, even if we may not be immediately aware of their messages. Additionally, reflecting on dreams helps individuals to remember their dreams; focusing on dreams improves the ability to remember dreams upon wakening.

To assist analysands, Delaney devised a Dream Interview Method through which a friend or professional, "who pretends to come from another planet,"[127] can question the dreamer. This "alien" identity avoids biases and creates openness so that:

> The would-be interpreter becomes an interviewer who will be
> curious to discover what life is like as seen through the waking

and dreaming eyes of the dreamer. Thus the interviewer tries to set aside any personal knowledge, beliefs, opinions, and associations regarding the images in the dream. The interviewer *asks the dreamer to define and describe* the images as if she were describing them to someone who had never heard them before... Meanwhile, the interviewer keeps her opinions and hypotheses to herself.[128]

Delaney also stresses the importance of having the interviewer restate the dreamer's descriptions and ask if they are accurate. Hearing one's dreams from another's "voice" allows the dreamer to bridge visual and verbal perceptions to create better understanding. Then the interviewer asks the dreamer to "bridge" the dream descriptions/elements to waking life. In the final summary stage, the bridging associations are also recapitulated, repeatedly, so the dreamer can reflect on these connections and deepen the resulting "feeling-rich" descriptions of each major dream element.

Reflecting upon dreams is an important step. To aid in this process, Delaney suggests dreamers diagram their dreams, just as one would diagram a sentence, and place each component in one of six categories: settings, people, animals, objects, feeling, actions/plots.[129] Additionally, she believes that outlining dreams is an effective way to help the dreamer recognize parallel situations and feelings, which in turn, facilitates the process of bridging dream elements to waking life experiences.

Gayle Delaney said that her goal is to help dreamers understand the metaphorical language of their dreams in order to link or bridge them to waking consciousness to effect healthier and more fulfilling lives. She asserted, most of her analysands report dreams that, when interpreted, can improve the quality of their lives.[130] To assist them in this healing process, she proposes a process of "incubation," wherein dreamers can control the content of their dreams to focus on their most pressing or perplexing issues. Simply put, a dreamer writes out a question, then repeats it when falling asleep. To Delaney, a professional eight-step procedure begins with first choosing the best night; one shouldn't be overly tired or under the influence of any intoxicant. Second, before sleeping, one should record "day notes," focusing only on the most important emotional highlights. Third, the analysand should examine the day notes closely, discussing them with one's "self" to allow the conscious mind to deal with the elements. The fourth step consists of composing a one-line "incubation phrase," the simpler the better. Next, step five consists of repeating this phrase over and over again while falling asleep. Step six is simply to sleep. Upon waking, step seven consists of recording all of the details of remembered dreams and emotional feelings, without making judgments. Last, step eight is to begin the interpretation process by using Delaney's Dream Interview Method.[131]

Delaney's "no nonsense," approach to dream interpretation is, as she phrases it, "a call to reality" and a means for dreamers to live healthier and more rewarding lives:

> My twenty-five years of study have convinced me that dreams are a call to reality and to living life courageously. Most of us live lives of quiet intimidation—in the big things, and especially in the little ones. When we listen to our dreams, which show us how we really feel and what we really think, when we let them nudge us to act on our insights, our lives get very interesting. I can think of no more exciting way to live, nor of one less suited to a passive acceptance of old formulas of interpretation or indeed of living.[132]

As Gayle Delaney asserts, understanding our dreams certainly does make life exciting.

And the more we get to experience it, the more exciting it becomes until eventually, we come to realize there is more to life than mere existence.[133] Dreams awaken us to this "more." Dreams connect us to our psyches, a word which stems interestingly from breath, indicative of the biblical revelation in Genesis that the breath of God animates the waters. However, doesn't God's mere act of animation suggest that the waters predate the Divine? Water is a timeless metaphor of the womb, a reference to Goddess spirituality. It is this breath to which psyche refers, the breath of the soul, not simply of the body. Psyche represents the totality of our lives or, most importantly, as Socrates posits in Plato's *Phaedo,* to the immortality of our souls released from, and unhindered by, the perishable confines of our transient bodies. Thus, through dreams, we travel back through the body from which our mothers birthed us— transcend the breath of life—to awaken to the eternal spirit that informs and animates our souls.

Chapter Three

DREAMS AND SPIRITUAL HEALTH

When did we begin dreaming? Were Homo Sapiens (circa 40,000 B.C.E.) truly the first human beings or, as the latest research suggests, were earlier hominids already leaving evidence of symbolic, dream-like awareness? Regardless of who these first dreamers may have been, their awakening to the spirit that informed and instructed them is the same awakening we experience nightly in our dreams.

The human spirit is eternal, and in our dreams we draw closest to the source of all being, including ours. As Wordsworth exclaims:

Our birth is but a sleep and a forgetting:
The Soul that rises with us, our life's Star,
Hath had elsewhere its setting,
And cometh from afar:
Not in entire forgetfulness,
And not in utter nakedness,
But trailing clouds of glory do we come
From God, who is our home:
Heaven lies about us in our infancy![134]

And Jung confirms:

Primitive man was much more governed by his instincts than are his "rational" modern descendants, who have learned to "control" themselves. In this civilizing process, we have increasingly divided our consciousness from the deeper instinctive strata of the human psyche, and even ultimately from the somatic basis of the psychic phenomenon. Fortunately, we have not lost these basic instinctive strata; they remain part of the unconscious, even though they may express themselves only in the form of dream images.[135]

One can only imagine how frightening yet miraculous it must have been for the first human beings to awaken from sleep and remember their dreams. How could they possibly tell the difference between the realities of waking life and the realities of their nightly visions? Was early human reality one unbroken, continuous stream? It must have been. For as Mircea Eliade suggests, there are moments when we can awaken to primitive intuitions of the sacred nature of life and what he terms the concept of "Great Time":

> ...[At such moments] modern, secular and thoroughly "historical" humanity dimly intuits something of the aboriginal feelings which prehistoric humanity evinced for the sacred dimension in life—for the experience of time not as a simple succession of linear moments, as it were, but rather as a replenishing epiphany of the archetypal time of beginnings, of the "Great Time" of sacred origins. The semantic roots of "holiday" (holy day) should suggest to us something of this "Great Time": the time which "makes us whole" as it soothes and heals our fractured consciousness—heals it, that is, until the alarm clock summons us back to something we choose to call the reality of a working week.[136]

Perhaps, we can find such moments of "Great Time" evidenced today in the behavior of children. Just recently, for example, while in a supermarket, I saw a young girl dancing and spinning around, oblivious to her mother's frantic hurrying to finish her shopping and to the myriad of other harried adults rushing past her in the aisle. The enchanted girl danced, sang and spoke aloud to no one, completely comfortable existing simultaneously in waking life as well as in her dreams. Now, how different is she from a young girl whose 17,000 year old footprints dating to the Magdalenian period of the Upper Paleolithic have just been identified in a remote Pyrenees cave? The footprints were previously believed to have been made by a number of individuals participating in some sort of ritual performance, but thanks to Namibian "trackers," they are now recognized as having been made by one dancing young girl "…[P]layfully pushing her feet into the soft ground. "[137]

This concept that life is a continuous dream state is echoed throughout humanity, in the West, for example in the words of Shakespeare's Prospero:
> We are such stuff
> As dreams are made on; and our little life
> Is rounded with a sleep (4.1.156-58).[138]

And it is echoed in the East as this often referenced epiphany of Zhuan Zhou (c. 369-286 B.C.E) illustrates:
> Once upon a time, I, Chuang Chou, dreamt I was a butterfly, fluttering hither and thither, to all intents and purposes a butterfly. I was conscious only of my happiness as a butterfly, unaware that I was Chou. Soon I awaked, and there I was, veritably myself again. Now I do not know whether I was then a man dreaming I was a butterfly, or whether I am now a butterfly, dreaming I am a man.[139]

As Marc Barasch relates, this enigmatic dream concept is echoed in Buddhist thought as well: "…I have been told by several lamas that dream yoga begins with recognizing the dream-like qualities of daily life—a practice known as *trekcho*. Here the practitioner is urged, upon waking up from a dream that just moments before seemed so real, to contemplate the similar insubstantiality of the daytime experiences to come."[140]

Carl Gustav Jung also recognized the connection of dreams to the source of our very being and as a means of awakening humanity to the reality of our "eternal" spirituality. Here, he eloquently illuminates the essential distinctiveness of dreams as doorways through which we can "awaken" to the sacred, transcendent nature of our "true" and "eternal" identity:

The dream is a little hidden door in the innermost and most secret recesses of the soul, opening into that cosmic night which was psyche long before there was any ego-consciousness, and which will remain psyche no matter how far our ego-consciousness may extend. For all ego-consciousness is isolated; it separates and discriminates, knows only particulars, and see only what can be related to the ego. Its essence is limitation, though it reach to the farthest nebulae among the stars. All consciousness separates; but in dreams we put on the likeness of that more universal, truer, more eternal man dwelling in the darkness of primordial night. There he is still the whole, and the whole is in him, indistinguishable from nature and bare of all egohood. It is from these all-uniting depths that the dream arises, be it never so childish, grotesque, and immoral. So flower-like is it in its candor and veracity that it makes us blush for the deceitfulness of our lives.[141]

What the Ancients Knew

Prehistoric Dream Visions

From the moment of their emergence, dreams have been simultaneously understood yet misunderstood. As a result, they are as much enigmatic as they are revelatory of the psyche's recuperative abilities or inabilities. As Hamlet's "To Be or Not to Be" soliloquy demonstrates, the promising solace of sleep may "end the heartache and the thousand natural shocks that flesh is heir to," but dreams are also most troubling because of the very uncertainty of their nature, "For in that sleep of death what dreams may come, when we have shuffled off this mortal coil, must give us pause" (*Hamlet* 3.1.62-66).[142] Yet in pursuit of any possibility of respite from waking life's "slings and arrows of outrageous fortune," we eagerly ponder the mysteries of our dreams despite their nightmarish potentiality—and we apparently have done so since the very origin of the human spirit. Citing the work of Johan Lind at Stockholm University in Sweden, Alison George summarizes Lind's surprising findings regarding the possible origin of hominid symbolic thinking, a prerequisite of dreams:

> Casting their net wide, Lind's team included data on the FOXP2 gene, which is thought to be associated with linguistic development, and changes in the vocal tract, as well as archaeological clues for things like fire use and complex tool technology—traits that should rely on the same "abstract" toolkit that gave rise to symbolism. In a paper published earlier this year, they estimated that the modern mind arose at least 170,000 years ago, and perhaps as far back as 500,000 years in an ancestor like H. erectus. "Things seen as uniquely human traits are deep in the phylogeny," says Lind.[143]

Consequently, in spite of any apprehension, our desire to understand our dreams and our belief in their curative potentialities can be traced to the earliest evidence of humanoid creativity. Indeed, one could say that, despite our fears of the unknown territory of dreams, our belief in their importance and healing nature is inherent in the figurative albumin of the human spirit, which long predates the advent of history and, as it now appears, even our species. As a result, our dreams are as beguiling as the alluring songs of Sirens, tempting us with their pleasurable promises yet harboring a sense of danger and destruction. But dreams tell us there is nothing to fear; this music *must* be heard, for when our eyes are cleansed, the destruction we dread proves to be the very essence, the *chi*,[144] of who we are. Through dreams, we awaken to the "self" and to the "selflessness" of connection to each other and to the source of all "being." This paradoxical message of our dreams is the same one our earliest ancestors tried to communicate to us through their art and artifacts, for it was also the essence of their dreams.

So why haven't we listened? What makes understanding prehistoric art so difficult? Like dreams, it is composed of metaphorical imagery and, therefore, can be ambiguous. Because waking life, that form of reality in which to our detriment we are far too perilously immersed, is composed of signs, not symbols, dreams and cave art are confusing. In waking life, a sign has a one-to-one designation, for example this sign: + (a plus sign). Whenever it appears in any equation, it always signifies the same thing: add. But this same sign in dreams becomes a symbol (a condensation) and as such, it can have a multitude of possible meanings. For instance, in Christianity, it represents the cross upon which Christ was crucified. In Native American culture, it demonstrates the four sacred directions of one's marked territory, a mapping process called land *nam*. To Australian aborigines, it is the earthly emergence point out of which humanity came and from which it spread. In Hindu art, it demonstrates how opposites can be one and the same, for simultaneously, it represents the process of evolution from a single point outwards while at the same time, it illustrates the subsequent devolution of all things returning from the periphery to the center. A stone tossed into the center of a pond creates waves that spread to the shores, but those same waves then progress back to the center from which they came. This complementary "wholeness" of opposites is also demonstrated by the Taoist coming together of *yin/yang* elements. Consequently, to understand dreams and prehistoric art, we must relearn what Erich Fromm called the "forgotten language" of symbolism because, as Jung asserts:

> The symbol-producing function of our dreams is thus an attempt to bring the original mind of man into "advanced" or differentiated consciousness, where it has never been before and where, therefore, it has never been subjected to critical self-reflection. For, in ages long past, that original mind was the whole of man's personality. As he developed consciousness, so his conscious mind lost contact with some of that primitive psychic energy. And the conscious mind has never known that original mind; for it was discarded in the process of evolving the very differentiated consciousness that alone could be aware of it.

> Yet it seems that what we call the unconscious has preserved primitive characteristics that formed part of the original mind. It is to these characteristics that the symbols of

dreams constantly refer, as if the unconscious sought to bring back all the old things from which the mind freed itself as it evolved—illusions, fantasies, archaic thought forms, fundamental instincts, and so on.[145]

Reunification with the "original" mind creates a spiritual wholeness which is itself "health." The word "holy" is from Old English, *halig*, akin to *hal* which means whole. Health and healthy also derive from *hal*—thus, holy and healthy mean "whole." When one awakens to spirituality, one atones (is "at one") with ultimate deity—one is whole. When one is healthy, one is also whole. A spiritual understanding of dreams attempts to reunite health and holy to make one whole. Dream metaphors, like prayers, bridge dream consciousness with waking consciousness to reveal the origin of human spiritual health. But is there evidence of such metaphorical thinking in prehistoric art?

Exactly when symbolic thinking evolved we may never know, but it appears in the earliest artistic expressions of *Homo Sapiens*. For example, Marija Gimbutas' studies of Old European art and artifacts brought her to recognize their symbolic communicative abilities:

> Some twenty years ago when I first started to question the meaning of signs and design patterns that appeared repeatedly on the cult objects and painted pottery of Neolithic Europe, they struck me as being pieces of a gigantic jigsaw puzzle—two-thirds of which was missing. As I worked at its completion, the main themes of the Old European ideology emerged, primarily through analysis of the symbols and images and discovery of their intrinsic order. They represent the grammar and syntax of a kind of meta-language by which an entire constellation of meanings is transmitted.[146]

And as Sigmund Freud posited, this symbolic, imagistic language also structures the "dream-work," especially regarding the processes of condensation and representation.

For example, just as a dream can present a multitude of images that appear to be incomprehensible but are juxtaposed to create a *mis en scene* conveying a message far "more than the sum of its parts," prehistoric art also appears to be chaotic and senseless, as evidenced by, for example, the enigmatic image of a bison-headed sorcerer dancing among a myriad of animal images superimposed upon one another in a chaotic jumble that decorates a sanctuary wall of the *Les Trois Freres* cave. But it is not. Once understood as an example of condensation, its message becomes quite clear: The dancing human shaman, adorned with animal hide and horns, is a representation of the interconnectivity of all life, recognized through participation in a dream-like hypnotic dance. This spiritual epiphany, that the killing and eating of animals is not destructive but transformative, both relieves the guilt of animal slaughter and consumption and simultaneously recognizes humanity's role as one piece of the great puzzle of all eternally renewing existence. Hence, the slaughtered beast sacrifices its life, so the hunter can live. Like Ouroboros (the serpent feeding on its own tail), life gives itself to sustain life in a never ending cycle of renewal, which encircles the entranced sorcerer clothed in the robes of sacrificial life.

From this perspective, the art and artifacts of our first ancestors can be readily perceived to be nonverbal emanations of prehistoric dream consciousness. Just as we do today, the fears and hopes and questions that confronted and confounded primitive humans during waking life were processed during their dreams. The non-REM cycles formulated strategies while REM dreams allowed them to safely explore any and all possibilities. Thus, dreams are the ultimate "survival tool," for without the ability to dream, humans would not be able to thrive in waking life. As a result, because our most ancient ancestors were more in touch with their dreams, primitive art expresses these REM dream possibilities in a way that is so much closer to "truth" than our dreams today for indeed, in this technological, increasingly isolating world, as Wordsworth laments, "We have given our hearts away, a sordid boon!"[147]

So how can we reconnect with the dreams of our prehistoric ancestors? An examination of their art offers help. For example, in *The Roots of Civilization*,[148] Alexander Marshack relates how he painstakingly examined markings on prehistoric bone and antler remnants, especially a bone fragment from the Aurignacian period (ca. 47,000 to 41,000 years ago), and determined that the etchings were neither random nor made at the same time. Rather, he realized they were systematic calendar notations based on the cycles of the moon; each mark was curved to emulate the night by night changes in the shape of the moon's arcs. These Cro-Magnon bone fragment notations are particularly important because the overall image created by the markings form the shape of a coiled serpent, perhaps a prehistoric precursor of the Indian Kundalini.

This juxtaposition of serpent with the phases of the moon is evidence of what Marshack termed "factored-thinking," a prerequisite for the formation of the symbolic nature of dreams. Simply put, factored-thinking refers to a systematic recognition of nature's cyclical patterns, an epiphany essential to the human ability to formulate analogies. As Freud realized very early-on in his research, dreams are symbolic communications, which speak to us in the analogical language of imagery. Therefore, this apparently simple image of a serpent-shaped calendar is both an intuitive manifestation of truth and an excellent example of dream condensation, whereby a multitude of meanings can be revealed through analysis. It is a silent bit of wisdom communicated from the deepest dream regions of our tripartite brain,[149] the reptilian core.

So what does this serpentine representation symbolize? From the earliest of cave art and artifacts through the ages, the serpent has been associated with the female. Merlin Stone reveals that despite its mistaken phallic identification, the serpent was primarily understood to be a feminine metaphor for spiritual "wisdom and prophetic counsel."[150] Early on, serpents were associated with Goddess mystery cults—long before any idea of male phallic prowess; for example, Python,[151] which coiled around the tripod stool of the priestess of the Oracle at Delphi, the Pythia, communicated the words of the Goddess. As Stone asserts, "According to Pausanius the earliest temple at this site had been built by women, while Aeschylus recorded that at this holiest of shrines the Goddess was extolled as the Primeval Prophetess."[152] These divinations were quite popular because "...[T]hese women were in direct communication with the deity who possessed the wisdom of the universe."[153] Furthermore, accessing the source of this wisdom was most likely the result of serpent venom, which created dream-like hallucinogenic effects, very much like mushrooms or peyote cactus, which brought Stone to speculate that the serpents were utilized as vehicles of divine (feminine) revelation.[154]

In fact, serpent imagery, illustrative of the Goddess as the true "Mother of Modern Medicine," predates contemporary male symbolism, such as the caduceus, by tens of thousands of years. Yet the caduceus is erroneously believed to accurately symbolize the medical field, perhaps because of the myth in which Hermes separated two fighting serpents with his wand, and in a show of peace, the serpents entwined around the staff to form the caduceus motif. Or perhaps it can be traced to the Roman legions' utilization of an olive branch wrapped with white linens, called the *caduceator*, to designate the presence of noncombatants on the battlefield. Nevertheless, Hermes is a completely inappropriate figure to represent health and healing:

> At his best, Hermes was overly shrewd; at this worst, he was an ingenious deceiver. Mercury, his Roman counterpart, became even more identified with commercial pursuits and was commonly depicted carrying a purse bulging with coins. In Homer's "Hymn to Hermes," Apollo is scathing in his assessment of Hermes: "This among the Gods shall be your gift...To be considered as the Lord of those who swindle, housebreak, sheepsteal and shoplift. A schemer subtle beyond all belief."[155]

To modern medical practitioners, be they physical, mental, or spiritual healers, the most disturbing role of Hermes has to be that of *psychopompos,* the guide to the underworld. Any profession devoted to saving and bettering lives would most certainly not want to be associated with hastening and facilitating their patients' journeys to death.

Furthermore, not only is the caduceus an inappropriate metaphor for healing, but also it has no real link to antiquity. The closest identification would be a seventh century C.E. connection with alchemy[156] which, itself, is a strong argument against its use as a reference to any healing arts: " The caduceus was the magic staff of Hermes (Mercury), the god of commerce, eloquence, invention, travel and theft, and so was a symbol of heralds and commerce, not medicine. The words caduity and caduceus imply temporality, perishableness and senility, while the medical profession espouses renewal, vitality and health."[157]

Actually, the main reason the caduceus is even remotely connected to health was its[158] use as a printing mark in the frontispiece of 17th and 18th century pharmacopoeias and its subsequent adoption by the United States Army Medical Corps (USAMC), on 17 July 1902, as their "golden" collar insignia to be worn by all medical personnel. However, this implementation was passed despite a great deal of opposition from protestors, who rightfully recognized it as a "misunderstanding of classical mythologic iconography."[159] At the time, even the Surgeon General, Lieutenant Colonel McCulloch, attested to the inappropriateness of the imagery: "I think that in this country we pay too little attention to the historical and humanistic side of things…The caduceus or wand of Mercury now used on the collar of the uniform blouse…of the medical corps, has really no medical bearing whatever…It really should be replaced as a corps design by the Aesculapian [sic] staff and serpent."[160]

As Lieutenant Colonel McCulloch suggests, the staff of Asclepius does have a connection to the medicinal practices of early

Greece and Rome, and as such, it presents a better argument for the association of the serpent with a male practitioner of the healing arts, but even this does not mean that it should in any way become emblematic of the *true roots* of modern medicine: the Goddess tradition of prehistory.

The staff of Asclepius differs from the Hermes' caduceus in that there is only one serpent entwined around a staff, and this image can be traced during the historical period to ancient medical practices, as it appears to be an illustration of a form of treatment used to rid patients of a type of filarial worm, *Dracunculus medinensis,* also know as "the fiery serpent," "the dragon of Medina," and the "guinea worm."[161] The worm would burrow under a patient's skin, so treatment consisted of cutting a slit in front of the worm's path to facilitate its ability to crawl out. Once the worm began to appear from out of the cut, the physician carefully allowed it to coil around a stick until it was completely removed. At that time, this infestation was so widespread that physicians would advertise by displaying signs painted with the image of a worm on a stick.

Because of this medical connection, the serpent became identified with Asclepius, who is described by Homer in the *Iliad* as a "blameless physician." Furthering the connection, when Asclepius was deified as a god, he assumed the form of a snake to cure the Romans of a terrible plague, and serpents also play a major role in one of his most defining healing moments, the resurrection of Glaukos:

> In perhaps the most popular tale, Asklepios is examining a man, Glaukos, whom Zeus had recently struck dead with a thunderbolt. During the examination, a snake gliding into the room surprised Askelpios, and he responded by killing it with a blow from his staff. Asklepios was subsequently intrigued by the arrival of a second serpent, which placed certain herbs in the mouth of the dead serpent and thereby restored it to life. Asklepios quickly perceived the lesson, revived Glaukos by recourse to the same herbs, and as a mark of respect, adopted the serpent coiling about his staff as his emblem.[162]

However, a close examination of this mythology brings us to an epiphany as to the identity of the true healer, the Goddess. Asclepius is *not* the healer. His association with serpents is an elaboration and purposeful altering of truth. As the myth clearly demonstrates, Asclepius simply learns from an earlier source of healing, the serpents, whose connection to the Goddess should be blatantly obvious, especially the epiphany that the very same herb that cures is also the poison that kills.[163] Utilizing the technique of Freudian dream displacement to refocus the healing power away from Asclepius and back onto the serpents redresses the elaboration and awakens us to the serpent power of life, death, and rebirth and, therefore, its connection to the Goddess. Just as the snake sheds its skin to be born again, the Goddess as "eternal feminine" gives birth, sustains life, and promises resurrection from death.[164]

In early history, Theriac, a veritable panacea of the ancient world, is a prime example of this enigmatic cyclical principle: extracted from snake venom, it had the potential to take or heal lives. It was extoled by Andromachus, who perfected the formula, and praised by Galen, whose belief in the venom-based concoction was sufficient to ensure its reputation even through the Medieval and Renaissance periods. The fame of Theriac actually resulted in the establishment of serpent farms to breed the very particular species of viper needed to make the elixir.[165]

The paradoxical nature of Theriac, importantly for this study, points us to the identity of the Goddess buried beneath the male serpent imagery. While Asclepius and other male deities focus almost exclusively on the curative aspects of medicine, the Goddess, as nature Herself, is recognized as the miraculous spiritual force that gives life, takes it away, and resurrects. The Norns (Germanic), for example, known as the Moirae (the Fates) in Greek mythology, presided over the life and death of each individual and even had power over Zeus, himself. And similarly, "the Egyptian snake Goddess *Meresger* could inflict disease on those who offended her yet was invoked to protect against snake bites. those who offended her yet was invoked to protect against snake bites."[166] As Christopher Lawrence concludes: "The association of the snake and medicine, with life and death, good and evil is thus no accident. It stands as a natural symbol of the most powerful forces in the cosmos….There is no reason…why we should not recast its old meaning in modern terms, for we are all very much aware that medicine today stands guard over some of the most powerful forces ever discovered by men and these…have the capacity for evil as well as good."[167]

The "natural symbol" of the "old meaning" can have only one reference: the Goddess. Essentially, this paradoxical nature—encompassing life and death, good and evil—eclipsed in history by male forces, is meticulously and variously represented in the dream-art of prehistory and thereby impossible to ignore. For the "eternal feminine" is indefatigable. Despite every attempt at obliterating Her existence, She is always just beneath the surface, like the buried wisdom bleeding through the fading overwriting of a worn palimpsest, because Her truth is an intuitive communication from dream consciousness, beyond reason—beyond doubt.

Thus, not so surprisingly, Merlin Stone's recognition of the healing importance of feminine spiritual wisdom in prehistory and this study's correlation of dreams with Goddess art representations are compellingly supported by contemporary studies in the field of brain physiology. This association of intuitive thinking and dreams is evident in female brain structure. Generally speaking,[168] male brains are about 10% larger and contain 6.5 times more grey matter; however, size does not matter in this case because women's brains have a number of advantages: They contain 9.5 times more white matter; the corpus callosum (the bridge of nerve tissue that connects the two hemispheres of the brain) is thicker; and the frontal portion and temporal area of the cortex are larger, more organized, and contain more volume than male brains. Therefore, the female brain is better equipped when it comes to analogical thinking, as women can more easily recognize and process spiritual, conceptual, emotional, and phenomenological "relationships."

Succinctly, women are much better symbolic thinkers. This is why I theorize in *Femina Sapiens*[169] that women were the first truly thinking human beings and that the majority of cave art and artifacts were very likely created by females.[170]

Furthermore, because of its metaphorical nature, a great deal of prehistoric art is dream-like in the sense that it demonstrates a Freudian "representational" connection of images, wherein one figure can be equivalent to, or turn into, another or even simultaneously, as in dream condensation, contain a myriad of diverse, dissimilar, and even complementary meanings. Therefore, in addition to womb imagery being expressed in serpent shapes, it can also be represented in cave art by trees, bucrania [bull head imagery], birds, water waves, and a number of other forms.[171] For example, early cave paintings often juxtapose tree imagery with lozenge-shaped womb symbols.[172] The message here is dream-like in at least a couple of ways. First, the minimalist abstraction of the womb as a lozenge shape with a single line is reminiscent of the poetic device, synecdoche, whereby the whole, in this case the Goddess, is represented by one of its parts, as in the "crown" for the king or queen or our "daily bread" for all sustenance. Second, the juxtaposition of the objects further mimics the dream-work process of "representation," in that it creates a simile, in this instance of functional equivalency. Just as the tree bears its produce, the womb gives birth to its fruit.[173] And more importantly is the epiphany of immortality: Just as the flesh of the fruit is sacrificed, buried, and resurrected, out of our death comes rebirth.[174] Prehistoric humans communicated this truth, but sadly fewer and fewer people in today's ever secularizing society are willing to accept this reality without skepticism. But without such an awakening to the dream wisdom of our ancient ancestors, how can we ever hope to achieve spiritual health?

Additionally, cave art is dream-like in the way it recreates the same message in differing ways,[175] for example, how the "eternal feminine" finds representational expression by what has come to be called the "*Venus of Laussel*" (see figure 1), a bas-relief, chiseled with primitive flint tools on an overhang of rock slanted above what may have been a long inhabited prehistoric sanctuary. Most impressively, the figure and its ground are masterfully intertwined: "Because the rock has a slight curvature, the figure seems to swell out of the cliff, emphasizing the pregnancy hinted at in the center of the image. Thus, this daily reminder of the 'mystery' that structures all life would be overwhelmingly displayed as a continual message to the inhabitants who sought shelter beneath its beneficent presence."[176] As a result, the image appears to swell out of the rock ledge, protruding outward in the middle then tapering down towards the feet, thereby drawing attention to the left hand resting on the pregnant fullness of the belly as if it were representing some sort of relationship between her swollen abdomen and the promise of life it contains with the crescent-shaped bull horn held aloft in her right hand.

The horn's crescent shape, reminiscent of the serpent, visually mimics one of the moon's four phases and, like the serpent-calendar, is also marked—in this case with thirteen stripes. Referencing Marshack's theory, like the serpentine-shaped bone markings, this too is a calendar. The thirteen incisions note the number of days from one crescent-shaped phase of the moon to the next. Since there are two crescent moons in one complete cycle from full to new moon, doubling the thirteen results in a total of twenty-six days. Adding the number of days the moon is actually in its full or new stages, the calendar becomes a fairly accurate recorder of the monthly female menstruation cycle. Thus, the message is a spiritual intuition that the heavenly cycle of life, death, and resurrection as paralleled by the moon's monthly rising and ebbing is clearly manifested in the womb of each and every female; each woman is herself a goddess. The universal power of the eternal feminine resides in all women:

Figure 1. *Venus of Laussel,* carved limestone block on rock shelter, c. 20,00-18,000 B.C.E. picture of original kept in Bordeaux museum, France.

...[T]here is the recognition that the life-giving powers of the Goddess are connected to the cyclical operations of the universe itself—a prehistoric awakening to the "as above, so below" conception. Additionally, by logical extension, there is the analogy of the Goddess to every woman. What the image seems to be implying is the Goddess is not some deity separate from its creation; rather, it is alive in every living thing. Furthermore, and more specifically, every woman is, ***herself***, the embodiment of the Goddess. And the Goddess is Herself visible in each and every woman. The monthly cycles each woman experiences are equivalent to the cycles of the moon, thereby equating her with the miraculous processes of an enigmatic, omniscient *female* universe.[177]

However, the *Venus of Laussel* depicts another important, perhaps quite surprising, connection: the juxtaposition of the Goddess with the bull horn. Though it suggests the serpentine crescent shape of a moon phase, it is undeniably a horn. Indeed, because of the object she holds in her hand, this enigmatic figure is often referred to as "The Woman with the Horn."

...[T]he Venus artist creates a relationship between horn and womb through utilization of the dream-work process of representation, where an equivalency of sorts is created by juxtaposition of the apparently diverse objects. The horn is held in one hand while the other hand, resting on the pregnant swell of the belly, points towards the pubic triangle. The metaphor is obvious: Horn and womb are synonymous. In fact, the shape of the horn itself is illustrative of the womb—just as it is of the cornucopia, a shell that symbolizes life in all its various forms entering the material realm from the Goddess in an eternal process of becoming and renewing. Like the conch shell cornucopia and the cowrie shell (associated with the womb because of its shape that resembles the "gate through which babies come"), the elongated cup-like structure of the horn is, quite possibly, the origin of the holy grail "chalice" that was in pre-Christian times a vessel, symbolic of the womb, which held—not the blood of Christ—the menstrual blood of the all-knowing Goddess. Indeed, the horn, the cowrie shell and red ochre were all synonymous with the perceived life-giving properties of menstrual blood, and more importantly with its powers of resurrection.[178]

In *The Chalice and the Blade: Our History, Our Future*, Riane Eisler explains the spiritual, tripartite healing nature of the Goddess, in that She not only gives and sustains birth, but also promises resurrection:

The main emphasis seems to have been on the association of woman with the giving and sustaining of life. But at the same time, death—or, more specifically, resurrection—appears to have been a central religious theme. Both the ritualized placement of the vagina-shaped cowrie shells around and on the dead and the practice of coating these shells and/or the dead with red ocher pigment (symbolizing the vitalizing power of blood) appear to have been part of the funerary rites intended to bring the deceased back through rebirth.[179]

Furthering the relationship between the womb and the horn reveals an extremely interesting connection. The bull horn is a synecdoche referring to the bucranium or shape of the bull skull and horns; as such, it shares a commonality of structure with the womb (see figure 2). Marija Gimbutas asserts that the incredible similarity between uterus and fallopian tubes and bucranium was an observation that prehistoric peoples would have been able to easily observe in the process of decaying death and burial. This identification to the Goddess womb made the bull horn a prominent symbol of "becoming," one which is meticulously evidenced in Neolithic art that illustrates the horns topped with ovarian stars or rosette shapes. As Gimbutas concludes, the metaphorical prominence of the bull is not a masculine identification;[180] rather, in this system of prehistoric art, "…[It] comes not from that

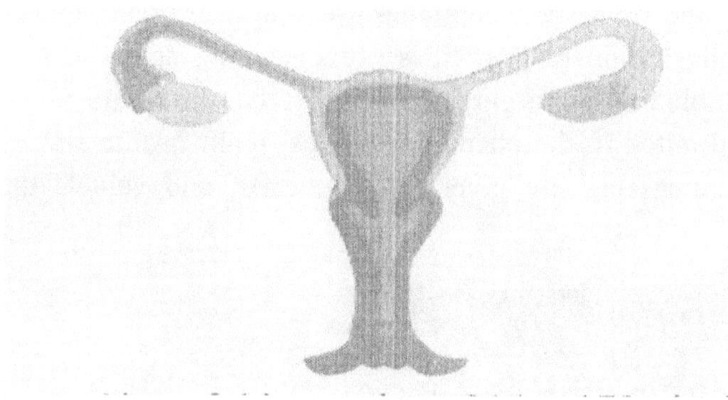

Figure 2. Artist's rendition of Bucranium shape of Female Reproductive Organs.

animal's strength and masculinity, as in Indo-European symbolism, but rather from the accidental similarity between its head and the female reproductive organs. The bull is not a god but essentially a symbol of becoming."[181]

The feminine process of "becoming" can be understood through the utilization of dream-work methodologies to analyze this shaman/bison image (see figure 3). The image presents a number of interesting points to explore: 1) the ithyphallic bird-headed shaman, 2) the bull pierced through with a spear, 3) the bird-topped baton, and 4) the spilling of the bull entrails.

Initially, the shaman was originally believed to be a victim of a tragic hunting accident, but even a rudimentary understanding of the primitive process of "magical thinking" disproves this idea: Our prehistoric ancestors would have never created this cave imagery for fear of its being recreated in the outside realm. Rather, it is far more logical to recognize the shaman as being in a dream-like trance. In this otherworldly state, he experiences an epiphany: There is a correlation between his erect phallus and the spear; in fact, their relationship is demonstrated by their juxtaposition. The trajectories of the phallus and spear fall on parallel lines, creating a simile—"this is like that." Just as the phallus in the womb creates and continues life, the spear (male) in the bull (female), spilling its innards, provides life sustaining nourishment. The male is responsible for discharging nourishment, but the female is its source. His role is limited to the phenomenological realm, while she is herself the all-encompassing life giver, life sustainer, and vehicle of resurrection.

Figure 3. Shaman/bison painting, Lascaux, c. 17,000 to 12,000 B.C.E.

But why is the shaman bird-headed, and why is his baton topped with a bird image? Simple. The birdman's role is to awaken us to the necessity of death in order to achieve resurrection. The epiphany is that out of the Goddess comes eternal life. Death is not the end of life; death is its opportunity to be born anew. But this awakening to truth must come from dreams; therefore, in his trance, the birdman is himself resurrected as female[182] by donning bird imagery.[183] Birds and serpents share a common ancestor, Archosauria, an identification well-fortified by recent archaeological research which strongly suggests that birds have evolved from dinosaurs. In true dream-work fashion, the bird imagery is an equivalent representation of serpent imagery. Birds, like modern-day illustrations of angels, represent spiritual beings, while the serpent connotes the corporeal self. In this drawing, not only is the shaman bird-headed, but also his baton is topped with a bird form. Could this be a prehistoric precursor to the caduceus symbolism, in which serpents and bird wings join together to represent the healing connection of soul atoned to body? Ultimately, only by adorning him/herself with Goddess images can the shaman awaken (ironically, through his deep dream trance) to truth: the promise of spiritual health through atonement with the Goddess.

But what has happened to this "truth"? Why has history been so cruel to the Goddess, the source of all physical, mental, and spiritual health? According to Leonard Shlain, the alphabet is the villain. In *The Alphabet Versus the Goddess*, Shlain connects the evolution of "literacy" with the demise of the Goddess. The advent of writing was the "death knell" of feminine metaphorical insights. Like dreams, as Shlain asserts: "Goddess worship, feminine values, and women's power depend on the ubiquity of the image. God worship, masculine values, and men's domination of women are bound to the written word... Whenever a culture elevates the written word at the expense of the image, patriarchy dominates. When the importance of the image supersedes the written word, feminine values and egalitarianism flourish."[184]

Hence, biblical history replaced "in the beginning was the womb" with "in the beginning was the word." The symbolism of the spiritually healing serpent became concretized and cursed as our greatest enemy:

> ...[C]ursed are you among all animals,
> and among the beasts of the field;
> On your belly shall you crawl,
> dust shall you eat, all the days of your life.
> I will put enmity between you and the woman,
> between your seed and her seed;
> He shall crush your head,
> and you shall lie in wait for his heel.

Genesis, 3, 14-15

But ironically, as science proves, nature abhors a vacuum. Disconnection from the healing source of our spirituality has created disillusionment with our waking world. Our unconditional beliefs in the rational powers of science and in the efficacy of ever warring male deities are now being challenged. The limits of medicine have been exposed by the onset of antibiotic-resistant diseases, fatally mutating viruses, and the return of once defeated illnesses. And the senseless violence and the tragic loss of life on a majestic scale by radicals invoking the names of their gods have created a desire for the "old time religion"—one of unity, of healing, and of promising resurrection. As a result, many today are reawakening to the prehistoric epiphanies of our earliest ancestors: Goddess cults, alternative health practices, and the importance of spiritual health are being freed from the repressions of our fearful egos. Our wellbeing and survival as individuals and as a species depends upon the messages of our dreams, for the body cannot be separated from the spirit or from its expressions. As Theresa Bertherat admonishes: ";Be wary of the body,' said a psychoanalyst who'd attended one of my classes a long time ago. 'Our bodies belong to the realm of the mother. When you approach the individual through the body, you enter directly into the archaic layers of the personality.'"[185]

Spiritual Dreaming in the Historic Era

History begins with words. Sadly, however, the alphabet has disconnected us from the prehistoric Goddess source of our dreams and their spiritual healing potential. It has moved us away from the recognition of our universal, metaphorical spirituality and toward a more concretized religious relationship with male deities, who provide more literal healing messages through dreams. As Leonard Schlain posits, "I propose that the central factor in the fall of the Goddess was a revolutionary development* which occurred during the same period—literacy. First writing, and then its more sophisticated refinement, the alphabet, tolled the death knell of feminine values both metaphorically and, as we shall see, quite literally."[186]

Succinctly, the stark rationality of written words replaced the symbolic nature of imagery. The experiential phenomenology of waking life eclipsed the metaphorical wisdom of dreams. The "all inclusive" connectivity of our spiritual selves gave way to individual, more personally precise efforts at healing the self, creating a "self" versus "others" mentality.[187] Nevertheless, the spirituality inherent in dreams cannot be so easily dismissed. Our desire to understand our enigmatic nightly journeys has withstood history and the ravages of time. As a result, hints of the spiritual healing potentialities of dreams are ubiquitously perceptible beneath the emphasis on a more literal interpretation found throughout the historical ancient world.

Sumerian

Among the "cradles of civilization," a suspicion regarding the prehistoric origins of dreams resides alongside the historic recognition that they are messages from the gods and as such, their interpretations are tied to religious practitioners. Consequently, professional dream interpreters were priests of sorts, who not only communicated the messages but also attempted to heal those who had "evil" dreams through a physical process of ritual cleansing.

In ancient Babylonia, there were dream interpreter-priests or "seers" called either *sha'il(t)u* or *baru*, who had the ability to tell the meaning of dreams and to take actions to avert their possible evil consequences. The first name means "he or she who asks questions [of the gods]." The second name probably derives from a verb (Sumerian *bur*, Akkadian *pasharu*, Babylonian *baru*) meaning "to unfold, explicate, set at ease," or in another sense, "to dissolve, dispel, destroy consequences."[188]

In an effort to preempt the evil consequences of dreams, the priest-practitioners transferred the malevolent dream content onto concrete objects, like clay statuettes, which could then be literally destroyed, thereby physically freeing the dreamer from potential harm. But as Hughes asserts, one would be mistaken to overlook the metaphorical, spiritual nature of this ritual: "When they "translated" the dream, revealing its symbolic message, the enigma of the dream disappeared, enabling the dreamer to find release through whatever prayer or other action the interpreter might prescribe, or which might be suggested by the purported meaning of the dream itself."[189]

Clues to the healing potentialities of dreams as symbolic, therapeutic emanations of Goddess messages can also be recognized in Mesopotamia (2,000 B.C.E.) by the iconography presented on a steatite libation cup of King Gudea of Lagash, which shows a "serpent god Ningishizzda as two snakes coiled around an axial rod."[190] This imagery is believed to explain the significance of Gilgamesh's confrontation with the serpent:

> Gilgamesh, an early legendary ruler of Uruk, dived to the bottom of the primaeval [sic] sea in search of the herb that bestowed eternal life. On his return he stopped to bathe. Meanwhile a cunning serpent stole the herb and, by casting off its skin, came into possession of eternal life. Man on the other hand was condemned to sickness and death. From then on the serpent was invoked as protector against disease. The myth of rejuvenation and its symbolic association with the snake's ability to shed its skin was almost ubiquitous in the ancient world.[191]

The significance of serpent imagery and its connection to the spirituality of the Goddess can be recognized by understanding that in dreams individuals attempt to reverse the psychoanalytic defense mechanism of reaction formation, which is itself an attempt to reverse destructive emotions to repress psychic suffering. Reaction formation occurs when the unconscious turns one concept into its opposite in order to defend against the painful truth: "This [reaction formation] is a mechanism whereby one of a pair of ambivalent attitudes, e.g., hate, is rendered unconscious and kept unconscious by an overemphasis of the other, which in this example would be love. Thus hate *appears* to be replaced by love, cruelty by gentleness, stubbornness by compliance, pleasure in dirt by neatness and cleanliness, and so on, yet the missing attitude persists unconsciously."[192]

Because the missing attitude persists, the reaction formation can be once again reversed, thereby revealing the serpent to be the rightful owner of the true source of eternal healing, the deep sea herb. Herbal healing, especially in the spiritual concept of resurrection of life, is the domain of the Goddess, and the serpent is Her iconic personification. Thus, in dream-like fashion, the Gilgamesh tale perhaps unknowingly relates the futile attempt at male usurpation of feminine spiritual healing, the herb in its aquatic womb, as symbolized by the metaphorical eternally resurrecting serpent triumphant over even such a powerful male as the demi-god Gilgamesh.

Furthermore, in the Mesopotamian period, the most likely candidate for the actual identity of the serpent-god Ningishizzda depicted on the libation cup is not male; rather, it is Ishtar, the source of all life, who was portrayed as a snake. Therefore, Gilgamesh may have defeated Ishtar to gain his worldly glory, but Ishtar, as the victorious serpent, maintains the otherworldly power of resurrection. Consequently, Gilgamesh's frustrating setback at the hands of the serpent is the reaction formation that awakens him to Her ultimate victory. The resurrecting powers remain with Her, despite all of his efforts to usurp Her dominion over them. Ishtar's identity, or at the very least the female identity of this serpent deity, is actually hinted at in the root of the name, Ningishizzda, which is feminine, not masculine: "Niggizzida was a deity...of the underworld and guardian to the entrance to heaven. Ningizzida, a feminine form of name, means 'lord of the good tree' in Sumerian and represents protection, medicine, magic and fertility. Ningizzida was sometimes depicted as a serpent with a human head, and was considered an ancestor of Gilgamesh."[193]

Ultimately, words may be deceiving, but the "forgotten language"—forever alive and revealed to us in the imagery of our dreams—speaks true.

Egyptian

Dreams in early Egypt were also regarded as messages from the gods, which often demanded dreamers to take physical action to either redress or prevent dire consequences or to execute pious deeds. As a result, they regularly played an important role in both politics and religion; hence, dream interpretation frequently promised godly rewards in the corporeal realm. Thus, as Gayle Delaney explains, many recorded Egyptian dreams tend to recall actual occurrences. She cites the dream of King Thutmose IV (1450 B.C.E.), who was promised a successful rule if he cleared away the sands that buried the Sphinx, and the dream of Tanutamon, who saw serpents "left and right," a symbolic understanding of which resulted in his ruling over the two Egypts: upper and lower.[194]

In Egypt, the interpretation of dreams required professional, highly educated, temple priests, since they dealt with portents of a spiritual nature as they manifested in the material realm, "…[T]emple priests [were] called 'Masters of the Secret Things' or 'Scribes of the Double House of Life' ('Learned Ones of the Magic Library'). As the names indicate, they were in charge of collections of papyri containing knowledge about omens, dream images, and the gods who had particular ability to interpret dreams and send good ones."[195] Consequently, through the stratagems of these priests, dreams could be incubated in order to petition the support of the gods regarding either the warding off of nightmares and the demons of the night or to request health-restoring, pleasant and spiritually calming sleep.

Nevertheless, perhaps the most interesting connection of dreams to spiritual health and eternal life can be found in *The Egyptian Book of the Dead*, where the waking world and the afterlife are recognized as continuous strands of existence, accessed through the passageways of dream and even death:

> ...[T]hese regions seem to blend together at points. They are places whose connection with this world often occurs on a liminal level, in sleep, dreams, visions, and death. In many senses, people encountered the next world in an altered state. The Egyptians' concept of the period between death and transformation in the next world strongly resembles their concept of the dream, in which one was awake while being asleep. For the Egyptians, the transformation into a soul or a spirit after death was an extension of this notion.[196]

In fact, as individuals progressed from waking life to death, priests guided the journey; they instructed them as if they, the deceased, were dreaming. "As in many other cultures, the Egyptian dead would be treated as if they were merely in a deep sleep and needed to awaken and go about their business."[197] Ultimately, through dreams as through death, Egyptians were not reborn; they were in a sense relocated—like emigrants moving from waking life through dream and death to the afterlife.

The Classical Period

The most famous of Greek dream healers was Asclepius, whose temples, most notably at Epidauros, Cos, and Pergamum, utilized the dream messages patients received from the god to diagnose and formulate health treatments. Afflicted individuals, guided by temple priests, would sleep among serpents, the symbol of the god, in the hope of receiving divine dream revelations that would awaken them to the possibility of potential curative therapies. However, the promise of physical wellbeing through a dream connection with the god is a misunderstanding of the true source of healing, the Goddess, as the temples of Asclepius are, themselves, references to the earlier nature cults: "Patients in Asklepion shrines also participated in rituals involving snakes, which were believed to be assistants of the healing god. Asklepios is frequently shown standing with a long wooden staff, around which is entwined a large snake. This staff, symbolizing the tree of life, and its coiling snakes represent the mysterious healing powers of the primal earth and are themselves remnants of pre-Grecian cults that worshipped the Earth."[198]

Again, the historical period's conception of gods as medicinal healers can be perceived as an effort to eclipse the spiritual healing powers of the Goddess, especially as they are revealed through dreams. However, because dreams are metaphorical in nature, their symbolism cannot be overshadowed. For example, three of the sons of Asclepius were doctors, but it is his five goddess daughters who reveal the feminine personality of spiritual healing. Hygieia, as her name suggests, personifies the "hygienic" qualities of cleanliness and health through sanitation. Aceso is the goddess who epitomizes the progression of healing itself, while her sister Iaso is the goddess who presides over the actual recovery process. The goddess of universal remedy, Panacea, is most emblematic of the Goddess' collective identity, from Whom we all come. And the goddess of beauty and magnificent splendor, Aglaea, represents the "attractiveness" of being whole and healthy, at one with the Goddess.

Prior to Roman occupation, in the fifth to fourth century B.C.E., the Amphiareion at Oropus rivaled the temples of Asclepius. Ailing and disabled pilgrims journeyed to the Amphiareion for both the promise of healing and for the oracular wisdom promised by the cult-hero/chthonic deity, Amphiaraus, who was recognized as a performer of miraculous cures. Amphiaraus was both a healer and a seer, whose patients were "expected to undergo a 'heightened' experience," for the god also delivered oracular declarations.[199] Under Roman aegis during the first century B.C.E., the health spa flourished again, partly thanks to financial support from Lucius Cornelius Sulla Felix, the Roman dictator-general. Its popularity continued throughout the period of the Roman Republic.

The site featured a sacred spring, through which it was believed Amphiaraus emerged from the underworld. Pilgrims were permitted to drink from its waters and, if cured, they would toss coins into the spring. Healing at the spa was mostly ritualized: After purification, pilgrims sacrificed a ram and slept upon its skin for either a cure or oracular advice from the god. However, the sacred spring and the sacrifice of the ram are, once again, revelatory of the true source of the Oropus sanctuary's healing powers: the Goddess. Here, Marija Gimbutas affirms the connection:

> The belief in the sacredness of life-giving water at the sources of rivers, springs, and wells extends from prehistory to this century. We still hear of Living Water which imparts strength, heals the sick, rejuvenates the old, restores sight, and reassembles dismembered bodies and brings them back to life. The cult of wells and thermal springs, especially those at the source of larger streams and rivers [as was the case at Oropus], cannot be separated from the cult of the life-dispensing Goddess, single or triple [in Her persona as life giver, sustainer, and resurrector].[200]

And, as Gimbutas explains, perhaps more interesting is the Goddess' identification with the ram:

> With the advent of animal domestication, it is not surprising that the ram emerges as a cult animal if one considers its importance to subsistence; sheep and goats account for 90% of animal bones found in Neolithic settlements. Its fleece provided warmth and its flesh nourishment.
>
> From the 7th millennium B.C. onward, ram figurines are marked with chevrons, parallel lines, snake coils, tri-lines, and nets. The ram continues to be identified as an animal sacred to the Bird and Snake Goddess throughout the Copper and Bronze

97

ages of Anatolia, the Aegean, the southern Balkans, Italy, and central, western, and northwestern Europe.[201]

Once again, the origin of the healing power of historical male deities—as manifested through dream interpretation—can be traced to the earlier prehistoric Goddess cults.

Judeo-Christian Era

The popularity of the Greek and Roman dream sanctuaries flourished for over a thousand years, through the Roman Republic, until their deposition by the ever increasing power of Christianity. As a result, ancient Jewish dream interpretation appears to have considerably drawn on the works of Greek and Roman philosophers, in the belief that dreams are prophetic messages from the gods, or in this case, from God.

The ancient Hebrews incorporated dreams heavily with their religion. The Hebrews were monotheistic and believed that dreams were the voice of one God alone. Also they differentiated good dreams (from God) and bad dreams (from evil spirits). They incubated dreams in order to receive divine revelation; for example, the Hebrew prophet Samuel would "lay down and sleep in the temple at Shiloh before the ark and the receive the word of the lord." The bible documents many prophetic dreams. Jacob, a Hebrew patriarch, dreamt of a ladder set up on the earth; the top of it reached to heaven and behold the angels of God ascending and descending on it; at the top of the ladder stood God. God promised Jacob that the land of Israel would belong forever to the Jewish people.[202]

Such a line of communication with the deity leads to the possibility that dreams could be incubated to petition individual responses from God, the only true source of healing.

This concept of dreams as instructions and guidance from God as communicated through a prophet practitioner reveals the fact that it is God alone who can bring about healing.

From the Jewish perspective, then, both physician and patient must acknowledge their dependence upon God: God alone ultimately delivers the cure or takes the life…Aside from the available medical treatments—which were pathetically limited and few—cures could come only from Yahweh by confession of sin, supplication, or prayer (e.g., Job 33:19-30). The Jewish approach to healing was therefore both scientific and religious, with God ideally leading the *rofe* (Jewish physician) to a higher understanding of the patient's plight.[203]

Nevertheless, the early Judean process of dream interpretation seems to have had more of a political role than a spiritual one, in that dreams were "authenticated" by connecting them to Scriptures, a process inherently subject to partisan manipulation:

In biblically oriented traditions, however, there was a need to show that dreams were really coming from God. Scripture could be used as a criterion for evaluating a dream as trustworthy. We think that in this period a certain strategy existed bringing together these forms in a divine revelation. In those stories where we find this strategy, the combination of dreams and Scripture guides the protagonist. Together these divine communications legitimate the protagonists' actions, often a crucial move within Judaism.[204]

As a result, it appears that legitimatizing dreams by connecting them to Scriptures often served to satisfy sovereign desires or political ends. Gayle Delaney points out that, in the Old Testament, in fact, there are at least two instances: first, Abraham's sleeping "in a high place" to hear God's proclamation that, though his (Abraham's) seed will be strangers in a foreign land, they will eventually find "great substance." And second, Solomon's sacrifices at Gibeon led to his dream, in which he asks God for an "understanding mind" to discern good from evil in order to successfully lead and judge His people.[205]

However, on a more personal level, dream healers may have played a larger role for Judeans, for although any form of necromancy was not religiously acceptable, the possibility that many Jews may have worked with more secular dream interpretation "specialists" cannot be dismissed too easily. Such encounters may have simply been banned from religious texts: "It may be that since dreams of spiritual encounters with God make such exciting, convincing, and educational reading for a large audience, the more personal, psychological dream work that may have been common was not included in most scriptures."[206] This may also be true of early Christians, who adopted the Jewish belief that dreams were prophetic messages from God. Christians also recognized that they could come from earlier Christian founders and disciples, or they could even provide revelatory glimpses into the God in one's heart—in the voice of perhaps one's "Guardian Angel"—as guides to proper living.

Early Christians had to accept the idea that at least some dreams had a divine inspiration. The bible mentions a lot about dreams and God communicated through them. The dreams of the New Testament were seen as straightforward messages from God, the disciples and other founders of Christianity. In the Old Testament, God declared that he would speak through dreams and visions and he said "hear now my words: if there be a prophet among you, I the LORD will make myself known unto him in a vision, and will speak unto him in a dream" (num. 12:6). Christians find dream[s] important because they believed that God chose to communicate through them. In dreams, they could see visions of the bible and God would grant them gifts and provide them with guidance. Dreams are reliable messengers. They reveal the condition of one's heart (Dan. 2:30) as well as the voice of God within one's heart (Acts 2:17). The bible says that when people wake up from their dreams, they act upon them.[207]

Among well-known early Christian examples of dreams as messages from God sent to awaken individuals to truth and action are Constantine's dream of a cross of light shining in front of the sun with the message: *"In Hoc Signo Vincis"* ("In This Sign You Shall Conquer"), and the dream of the three wise men, in which they were warned not to return to Herod after finding the Christ child.

But for most Christians in the ancient world or for even such renowned dreamers as Pharaoh and Nebuchadnezzar, these dream messages were often perplexing and difficult to understand and, therefore, required professional guidance.

The ancient world and the biblical tradition knew about dreams. The ancients understood that the unbidden communication in the night opens sleepers to a world different from the one they manage during the day. The ancients dared to imagine, moreover, that this unbidden communication is one venue in which the holy purposes of God, perplexing and unreasonable as they might be, come to us. They knew too that this communication is not obvious. It requires interpretation.[208]

Clearly, consulting a dream analyst is a procedure Pilate should have followed when he, instead, disregarded his wife's painful nightmare, cautioning him to have nothing to do with Jesus, a "just man."

However, despite this need for dream interpreters, during the first three centuries of Christianity, healing practitioners had to compete against the earlier pagan sanctuaries as well as institute their own belief system in response to the popular demand for religious healing. As a result, in Gary B. Ferngren's opinion:

"Christianity was not a religion of healing par excellence but underwent a curious process before becoming concerned with physical healing also." According to his [Ferngren's] reconstruction of these stages, Christian miraculous healing in the second and third centuries was, from the point of view of what was soon to become Orthodox Christianity, rather on the sectarian or heretical fringe, practiced by the Montanists, the Gnostics and the Carpocratians. The third century brought increasing emphasis on supernatural healing and the influence of demons, while the fourth witnessed a dramatic crescendo of all sorts of supernatural thaumaturgict [referring to the workings of magicians] techniques.[209]

Therefore, it was not until the later part of the fourth century A.D. that Christianity transformed into a healing religion—thanks to the ritualistic role of the Eucharist, a ceremony of Goddess' resurrection, as the means to communion with Christ. Here, Lldiko Csepregi explains Ferngren's philosophical reconstruction of this process of metamorphosis:

> Ferngren plausibly argues that the incorporation of bodily cures and Christianity's turning into a healing religion in the fourth century, accompanied by a "revolutionary change in the attitude towards the sick," was strongly tied to the urge to "compete with Asclepius on his own ground," as well as providing an adequate response to a powerful demand of the time: the need for miracles—mostly healing miracles. The fierce competition with the popular pagan healers is well reflected within the incubation collections, while the initial flourishing of Christian incubation in the period from the fourth or fifth to the seventh century witnessed the formation and struggles of Orthodoxy (or various orthodoxies) as well. By analyzing a small but significant group of dream-healing miracles in which the Eucharist plays a central role, I would like to illustrate the simultaneous presence of the motifs mentioned above: the ancient Greek legacy of incubation; the recognition of the saints' authority; the punishment miracle; the role of Greeks, heretics, skeptical intellectuals and unbelievers; the curative function of sacred acts; the theological context and hagiographical role of Communion in miraculous healing. Like

other ritual instructions in miraculous healing, the saints demand that patients take the Eucharist functions as a condition of obtaining health. Apart, however, from being a condition of healing, the Eucharist often becomes the chief issue, to which even healing is subordinated.[210]

By the fifth century, A.D., the Eucharist—as veiled throwback to prehistoric understanding of resurrection through the Goddess—enabled the healing practices of saints to eclipse the earlier Greco-Roman temples by insisting upon the health of the soul, purified through communion, as prerequisite to the healing of the body.

Faith and healing interact and reinforce each other. Miraculous physical recovery either leads the patient to convert or strengthens his existing faith; in other cases, the healers refuse to grant a cure unless the soul is healed beforehand. Miraculous healing was a tool in the hands of the saints or, rather, their hagiographers. The fact that the incubation cults of Saint Thecla, Saints Cosmas and Damian, and Saints Cyrus and John replaced influential pagan cults on the same sites demanded that the new healers prove that their miracles were more efficient than those of their predecessors.[211]

Through displacement of the resurrecting power of the Goddess onto the miraculous ritual of the Eucharist, saintly dream practitioners in Early Christianity eclipsed prehistoric spirituality to depose their pagan predecessors and establish themselves as the dominant spiritual healers.

China

Although there exists a great number of references to dreams and their various interpretations, specific works focusing predominantly on dreams in ancient China are not common. An example of such a text, however, would be *The Book Duke of Zhou Interprets Dreams* (3,000 B.C.E.), in which the cultural hero Duke Zhou (*Zhou Gong*), who is also credited with the writing of the *I Ching,* provides seven different categories of auspicious and inauspicious dreams, only one of which is on spiritual messages. Nevertheless, the popularity and admiration of this work is evidenced by its ubiquitous appearance in contemporary Chinese households. Even such an esteemed figure as Confucius is cited in his *Lunyu* (*Analects*) referencing the Duke of Zhou as the god of dreams: "One of the earliest Chinese references to dreams was reportedly made by Confucius in the fifth century B.C.E.: 'It's just too much,' he lamented near the end of his life, "' am declining. It has been a long time since I have seen the Duke of Chou in my dreams.'"[212] According to Chinese legend, any time there is the possibility of something important happening in one's life, it is believed that the Duke of Zhou will appear in one's dream, thus clarifying the meaning of the Chinese idiom "Dreaming of Zhou Gong," as admonishment of the need for attention.

Thus, it appears that guidance or demands from the afterlife eclipse the spiritual healing nature of dreams, for such dream visitations can also be noted during the Shang Dynasty, around the second millennium B.C.E., when dreams were believed to be communications with honored deceased ancestors, who often appeared demanding appeasement in order to avoid divine punishment. "In general, the Shang people seemed convinced that dreams were caused by the dead, in particular the *hsien-kung* and *hsien-pi*, that is, the patriarchal and matriarchal ancestors, whose ghosts were requiring propitiations by sacrificial offerings."[213]

This idea of a "dual soul," one that exists in life and another capable in death of communicating through dreams, is important for a couple of reasons. First, it strongly supports the potential of incubating dreams for purposeful communication with ancestral spirits to affect personal wellbeing: "If spiritual beings may on their own initiative manifest in dreams for whatever reasons, it is also the case that they may be deliberately induced to appear in dreams through prayer and/or some form of propitiation."[214]

As a result, dream incubation was also recognized in ancient China as a means of attaining wisdom through the appeasement of spiritual sources, just as it was in the Greco-Roman and Judeo-Christian eras. And just as in the West, dream incubation shrines were popular destinations, especially such sanctuaries as *Chiu-li* (Nine Carps), *Hsien-men Tung* (Cave of the Immortals' Gate), and the Temple of *Ch'eung-huang* (God of Walls and Moats).[215]

Second, the Chinese belief in the duality of the soul, which can be integrated with the universal concept of *Yin-Yang*, can also be recognized in the Egyptian conception of a multifaceted soul, most notably comprised of the *Ba*—associated with the essence of a being which exists after death—and the *Ka*—the vital essence for life, whose exiting of the body causes death.

Ultimately, in ancient history, the more than remarkable commonality of understanding how we interact with dreams in both the East and the West strongly suggests the possibility that cosmological synchronicity is an inherent quality of healing dreams. As the enlightened vision of Carl Gustav Jung has instructed us, through dreams we indeed awaken to the truer eternal self—and thereby atone with our collective, universal psyche.

"Living" Dreams and Myths

Jung defined dream as "a little hidden door" opening the way to the deepest levels of the psyche, and in *The Mythic Image*, Joseph Campbell utilizes the same symbolism to explain the equivalency of dreams and myth, "through dreams a door is opened to mythology, since myths are of the nature of dream, and that, as dreams arise from an inward world unknown to waking consciousness, so do myths, so, indeed, does life."[216] Campbell believed that "truth" is revealed through myth and dreams, for scientific outcomes of exploration are limited by their reliance on sensory input: ""Anything perceived by the waking senses, furthermore, must already have come into being, and so is already a thing of the past. Science, the wisdom of the mind awake, and of 'hard facts,' can consequently, be a knowledge only of what has already become, or of what in the future is to repeat and continue the past. The unpredictably creative, immediate present is inaccessible to its light".[217]

Thus, through myth and dreams, for they are truly equivalent, one can understand the spiritually healing powers of the "activating forces" that inform and inanimate our souls:

Mythologies are in fact the public dreams that move and shape societies; and conversely, one's own dreams are the little myths of the private gods, antigods, and guardian powers that are moving and shaping oneself: revelations of the actual fears, desires, aims, and values by which one's life is subliminally ordered. On the level, therefore, of Dream Consciousness one is at the quick, the immediate initiating creative *now*, of one's life, experiencing those activating forces that in due time will bring to pass unpredicted events on the plane of Waking Consciousness and be there observed and experienced as "facts."[218]

Consequently, the exploration of mythologies is a spiritual awakening to the healing source of dream consciousness and a valuable addition to intuitively discerning the divine manifestations of the collective unconscious. Through the correlation of myth and dream, we can understand the therapeutic power of human spirituality.

Perhaps, a revelatory sense of the dream/waking continuum of our earliest ancestors can best be found among the ancient mythologies of Australian aboriginals, to whom "creation" was "The Dream Time," a time when all past, present, and future were one—in a continuous moment of existence. Accessible through the altered state of dream consciousness, Dream Time transcends spatial and temporal existence and experience; as a result, in it, one becomes "at one" with all one's ancestors in an unbroken, undifferentiated state, the awareness of which originated in the dreams of the first creators, "All Father" in southern Australia and "All Mother" of northern Australia. Although the "myths of the ancestral Dream Time are known to all of aboriginal Australia,"[219] specifically, among the Unumbal of Northern Kimberley, creation is itself the product of a dream as the following myth recounts: "   In   the beginning, there were only Sky and Earth: dwelling in the earth was Ungud [All Mother], in the form of a great snake; and in the sky, Wallanganda [All Father], the Milky Way. Wallanganda threw water on the earth; Ungud made it deep. And in the night, as Ungud and Wallangada dreamed, life arose from the watered earth in the forms of their dreams."[220]

Indeed, all over the "watered earth," humans have been and are dreaming, and their dreams—despite their expansive proliferation throughout time and place—appear to come from a common collective, universal source, beyond reason—beyond the self. As a result, this same "power of myth" and its identification with dreams can be realized in the "living" mythologies of peoples all over the world, especially for example in the art of Indian Asia.

Hindu

The allegorical imagery of the mythic "Vishnu Dreaming the Universe" (see figure 4) depicts the dream-time continuum and the relationship of dream consciousness to the mythological importance of the intonation of AUM. From the sleeping god's naval, a lotus rises up to support Brahma, the lord of light, whose four faces illuminate the four corners of the material world. Vishnu, himself, is asleep upon the multi-headed serpent Ananta ("unending"), the personification of psychic energies. Vishnu's wife, Sri Lakshmi ("Beauty and Good Fortune"), who is also called Padma or "Lady Lotus," represents the universal, primary creative power or *"Shakti"* of the god's dreaming state. This "virtuous Indian wife" massages her husband's leg to stimulate his cosmic dream.

It is important to note that, although Vishnu dreams the universe into and out of existence, the actual progenitor, "Brahma" or Brachman (as differentiated from the Brahma sitting on the lotus growing from Vishnu's navel) is the "all creator" transcending the pairs of opposites, as he "whom words cannot touch." However, the displacement of Padma in this imagery is evident. Though relegated to a subservient role she, as *Shakti,* is the spiritual "creative force" usurped by Brachman, and she is the support, the lotus, upon which the waking world rests. Yet again, with the advent of the historical period, the Goddess is eclipsed by male personifications.

Portrayed in much smaller scale below Vishnu, the five Pandava brothers [221] (purposefully carved in diminutive stature to the gods above) demonstrate here the subservient nature of consciousness. Each brother represents one of the five senses. The brothers are collectively married to, and commonly share, the same wife, Draupadi, who symbolizes the brain or waking mind. Thus, the Pandava brothers and Draupadi exemplify the process of rational thought as a determination of sensory input. They are diminished in size to illustrate their inferiority. "Thus, the message here is the mind and its senses are a secondary, supportive function of the deity, generated from the 'divine continuum' and by no means its source or controlling factor. Consequently, portrayed in this simple yet profound imagery is the relationship of the layers of consciousness to the cosmic abyss from which they come, to which they come and to which they return."[222]

Figure 4. Vishnu Dreaming the Universe, Indian Relief, Deogarh, India

Likewise, in the "heavenly" plane above the sleeping Vishnu, Brahma is surrounded by other deities, notably Shiva and Parvati on his right and Indra on his left. They too are smaller in size than the central image. 0Therefore, the viewer is to perceive Vishnu as the "all generating" center from which all else, heavens and earth alike, diminishes in comparison. Ultimately, gods and humans emanate like dreams from the unconscious, then dissolve back into it like ripples animating a still pond, silently, or rather with the "unheard" music of the cosmic AUM, that sound which is made without the vibration of one thing against another.[223]

The essential equivalency of AUM to dreams is explained by Heinrich Zimmer, in his elucidation of the "syllable of four elements": "The whole form, finally, may be read as the mystic syllable OM or AUM…which is the totality of the world and psyche in the four states of awareness known as (1) being awake, (2) being in dream, (3) being in dreamless sleep, and (4) being reintegrated in the pure, transcendental essence of divine reality. Each of these four states is expressed in one of the four parts of AUM: respectively in *a, u, m,* and the following silence."[224] Discussing the significance of AUM, Joseph Campbell refers to it as the sound of the "void." AUM is antecedent to and anticipates everything. It can be heard from within as well as without.

The "four element" allegory is illustrated by the imagery of Vishnu's dreaming of the universe. The four directions of the "visible" world, as illuminated by the panoramic orientation of Brahma's four faces, represent the waking realm of gross matter symbolized by "A." In this world, A cannot equal not-A—that is, an apple cannot be something other than an apple. And like all apples, everything is perishable and subject to constant change.

To further the analogy, the "U" as the state of dream consciousness is composed of "subtle" matter, able to change form like the dreams of Vishnu who is, at once, dreaming yet at the same time a part of his dream. Reality is immaterial. Subject and object may appear differently and separately but are actually "one." For example, a dreamer watches his or her creation, yet simultaneously acts in and observes the dream—experiencing, in essence, both objective and subjective perspectives. In dreams, A is equal to not-A.

If "A" is waking consciousness and "U" is dream consciousness, then "M" is deep dreamless sleep wherein all temporal and spatial realities (A and not-A) are obliterated. The psyche is undifferentiated from, yet lost to, itself—awakened to an enlightened darkness. This is represented by the overwhelming incomprehensibility of the background blackness that enigmatically serves to make visible the foreground imagery.

So what, then, is the fourth element? It is the "silence" of the metaphorical "void" from which AUM comes and to which it returns. In Indian art, gods (for example Krishna, an avatar of Vishnu) are blue-black in reference to this figurative void, which is simultaneously their (and our) origin and ultimate destination. It is the "all" from which the image emerges like a momentary bubble on the surface of a pond—to which it once again "becomes."

This understanding of the connection of AUM to dreams is an epiphany that can also be revealed in the imagery of *Shiva Nataraja,* *"Lord of the Cosmic Dance"* (see figure 5). In *The Mythic Image,* Joseph Campbell explains the symbolism of the dancing god.[225] In his right hand, Shiva holds an hourglass shaped drum signifying the beat of time, which "draws a veil" over eternity. In his left, he holds the spiritual flame to burn it away. His inner hands form the "fear-dispelling" posture (with palm upraised) and what is called the "elephant hand" (raised across his chest) that signifies imparting wisdom, for the elephant clears a wide path through the density of the jungle on which anyone can then journey. The message, as in the *Upanishads* ("to sit down near"), is to not fear being close to a teacher for spiritual enlightenment. Shiva's left foot is lifted representing "release" (as if from gravity), while his right foot stomps upon a dwarf, "forgetfulness," whose fascination with the poisonous serpent bonds him to suffer imprisonment in the unending *samsara*, the cycle of worldly reincarnation.[226]

Juxtaposed to the frenetic movement of the dance as illustrated by the streaming dreadlocks of his hair, Shiva's head is still and his expression is serene, suggesting the complementary nature of opposites mysteriously coming together to form a whole "bigger than the sum of their parts." This metaphor is furthered by the *makara kundala* (fish-like) male earring in his right ear as differentiated from the *patra-kundala* (circular scroll) female earring in his left, symbolizing the god's transcendence of opposites. In his hair is a skull, a crescent moon, a datura flower (an intoxicant), and an image of the river goddess Ganges.

Again, the displacement of the Goddess as the source of "truth" can be recognized and redressed by analysis of the imagery. According to myth, Shiva's hair breaks the commanding fall of Ganga from crashing and devastating the earth. Ganga's "vanity" was thereby broken and made subservient to a male deity. In this, she is reminiscent of the early Jewish myth of Lilith.[227] Lilith was created at the same time and from the same earth as Adam, so when she was asked to be subservient to him, she refused and abandoned Eden. As a result, she has become demonized. Ganga's submission, on the other hand, relegates her to a displaced, diminished position in this iconography.

Additionally, as this image illustrates, fascination with the serpent as symbol of the Goddess entraps us in the birth, life, death, rebirth cycle of the "eternal feminine," in contrast to the promise of immortality through atonement with male gods. This same imagery can be seen in the Garden of Eden, where Eve and the serpent (as metaphors of the Goddess) tempt Adam (representative of humankind) to "fall" from the eternal, unchanging garden of the Father and, thereby, suffer the tortures of life and death.

Importantly for this study, Campbell concludes by recognizing the symbol of four elements, AUM, in the dancing posture of Shiva: "From the mouths of a double-headed mythological water monster called a makara the flaming aureole issues by which the dancer is enclosed, and the posture of his head, arms, and lifted leg within this frame suggests the sign of the syllable OM [AUM]...."[228]

The dream-like condensation of Shiva and AUM is the structuring force of this imagery, as with a little imagination, the Sanskrit word for AUM (see figure 6) can be easily transposed over the image of *Shiva Nataraja*, such that the god himself is the personification of AUM: In essence, AUM dances upon the dwarfish ignorance of our intoxication with waking reality, which blinds us to the healing spiritual truth of our dreams. The progression through all four of AUM's elements awakens us to the healing nature of the silence from which "truth" comes and to which it returns and from which it reemerges.

Figure 5. *Shiva Nataraja Lord of the Cosmic Dance* from Thanjavur Palace.

Figure 6. AUM.

Additionally, it is important to understand the role of *samsara,* the cycle of reincarnation, in contemporary Indian dream interpretation. It is a "given" and a starting point, for the belief in *karma*, the concept of one's intent and actions influencing future reincarnations, is still very strong. It is also imperative to note that the caste system is another factor that influences the meaning of dreams. For example, if a member of the Brahmin class, an individual from the *varna* or "pillar" of society—such as priests, teachers, artists, and professionals—dreams of acquiring more fertile land, this acquisition would be viewed as auspicious and deserved. In contrast, if a member of the "untouchables" (the *Dalit* or "polluting" community) has the same dream, this would be interpreted in a negative way, perhaps predicting dire consequences for overreaching the caste structure. Similarly, the geographical location of the dreamer is also noteworthy. The dream symbolism of a city-dweller would be interpreted differently from the same dream of a farmer or of one who lives in jungle areas. For example, a farmer who dreams of gathering more land might be wishing for a "boon" harvest; whereas, a businessman in Mumbai might be dreaming of distancing himself from city stresses. Nevertheless, in India, the concepts of reincarnation and *karma* still remain deep-seated central factors when interpreting dreams, as they do throughout the East among practitioners of Buddhism, which originated with the teachings of Siddhartha Gautama, in India.

Buddhism

According to legend, circa 400 B.C.E., in the Bodh Gaya region of India, Siddhartha Gautama "awakened" after forty-nine days of meditating beneath a Pipal tree, which has now come to be known as the Bodhi tree. His enlightenment as the Buddha ("Awakened One") resulted from his attainment of *nirvana,* which literally means to be "blown out" like a candle. *Nirvana* is the "extinguishing" of personal identity in order to escape from entrapment in the reincarnation cycle of *samsara.* As such, it can be compared with the fourth element of AUM, the silence from which waking, dreaming, and deep dreamless sleep come and to which they go. This comparison of the Buddha's intuitive, revelatory mediation and our nightly dream states should not be overlooked. For example, what is most interesting but often unnoticed is the importance of recognizing and redressing the dream-work displacement of the role of the tree, which should not be misunderstood as merely the background setting to the Buddha's enlightenment; rather, the Pipal tree of his awakening and the Sal tree under which he is born should be acknowledged as its source, his *Shakti.* Remedying the displacement is imperative because mythologies, like dreams, are metaphorical, so to concretize dream symbolism is to lose the spiritual message and fall victim to the delusory temptations of Mara, Buddha's tempter.

First, Siddhartha Gautama's birth under a Sal tree is itself the result of a dream. His mother, Queen Mahamaya ("Beautiful"), had a very vivid dream in which she is ritualistically bathed and purified before a white elephant carrying a lotus in its trunk enters her womb through her right side. The actual pregnancy resulting from this "virgin birth" culminates when the future Buddha is born from her right side, while she is holding onto the branch of a Sal tree. The symbolism here should not be ignored. The Sal tree represents the coming together of opposites because in dry climates, it is an evergreen, but in wetter areas, it is deciduous. Second, the Pipal tree under which Siddhartha Gautama achieves Nirvana is also metaphorical. It is a fruit-bearing fig, in this case engendering the "fruit" of his awakening to enlightenment.

Ultimately, recognizing the importance of tree imagery reawakens one to the Goddess power lost beneath the displacement of this concretized mythology. In meditation, the Buddha awakens to the same dream-like epiphany of our most primitive ancestors. The prehistoric cave drawings juxtaposing trees and vulvas are enlightenments of the same Goddess source of Nirvana—the extinguishment of personal identity—and atonement with the primordial cosmic energy, the dynamic force—*Shakti*—that informs and animates the universe. This is why, after transcending the pair of opposites—desire (in the form of beautiful women) and fear (from the wrath of attacking armies)—that Devaputra Mara (chief of all demons) uses to tempt him, the Buddha must then prove his worthiness for "awakening," which he does by touching the earth, the Goddess.

Mara's role as demonic tempter is to bring about the death of spirituality by alluring humanity with the mundane objects of the corporeal realm. As such, he parallels the serpent that fascinates the foolishly deluded materialistic dwarf upon whom Shiva, as "Lord of the Cosmic Dance," tramples and the infamous serpent in the Garden of Eden. The Buddha resists these temptations, but Mara still blocks his awakening by declaring that the Buddha has no witness to his claim of experiencing enlightenment, but when the Buddha touches the earth, she proclaims herself to be his "witness." Obviously, then, the Goddess was there at the Buddha's enlightenment—how else can she be a witness?

This is problematic because, to me, it questions the Buddha's achievement of *nirvana.* First, achieving *nirvana* requires the "extinguishment" of everything, including the self and all deities. But earth was not extinguished, for she was there. And if she witnessed his being there, she saw him as a being, a "self." Second, is not the Buddha's desire for release from suffering through *nirvana* itself an example of desire and fear? Desirous for extinguishment from suffering and fear, the Buddha seeks *nirvana.* But his motivation is itself a desire, in this case for *nirvana* to escape the "fearfulness" of suffering. Therefore, as I see it, this myth is another illustration of the first awakenings of human spirituality expressed through the dream-like imagery of prehistoric art, that it is through atonement with Her that one awakens to the ultimate spiritual truth. In dream-like mediation, Siddhartha Gautama awakens to the true Goddess source of AUM and assumes his identity as the Buddha.

Thus, through a basic application of dream-work methodology, the displaced Goddess metaphors of tree and earth are brought back into principal focus. It is under the Bodhi tree that the Buddha awakens, and his right to this place beneath the tree is affirmed by the earth. In the myth, when all else fails, Mara claims that he has more right to the seat at the base of the tree than does the Buddha, and Mara's armies attest to his right as a supreme spiritual being. But as his name suggests, Siddhartha does have this right. His name means one who has achieved what he sought, the meaning of existence.[229] And it is the Goddess who attests to this right. Is this not why, for one week after Siddhartha awakens, he stares with gratitude at the Bodhi tree? Interestingly, is this tree not reminiscent of the Norse *Yggdrasil,* upon which Odin sacrifices himself to himself to achieve enlightened wisdom? And like the trees which are metaphors of the Goddess earth in Buddhist mythology, *Yggdrasil* survives the destruction of everything including the gods post Ragnarok to regenerate all life again. Thus, an understanding of dream displacement redresses the usurpation of the Goddess tree imagery and provides valuable insight.

This interpretation of the myth as dream challenges the Buddha's rejection of desire and fear and the achievement of *nirvana* through the extinguishment of the self. To briefly reiterate, first the Buddha's quest is for the meaning of existence to escape the sufferings of life and, thereby, escape entrapment in *samsara*. This quest is itself a desire, and it is one that is motivated by fear. Second, the self cannot be extinguished if another can recognize it, which the Goddess does through Her witness. From the perspective of this dream, the Buddha does not reach *nirvana*; rather, he achieves the goal of his quest, to understand the meaning of existence through awakening to the Goddess' concept of all life as perpetual. Perhaps this is why Buddhism refutes any acceptance of a perpetual self. In *Sleeping, Dreaming, and Dying,* the Dalai Lama discusses the importance of "the basic foundation of the entire Buddhist doctrine," the Four Noble Truths and how understanding this principle pertains to health, happiness, and suffering: "The Four Noble Truths are often expressed in the form of four statements: recognize the Noble Truth of suffering; abandon the Noble Truth of the source of suffering; accomplish the Noble Truth of cessation of suffering; and cultivate the Noble Truth of the Path. All of this is to be done by the individual who seeks happiness and wishes to avoid suffering."[230]

Recognizing the source of suffering is to awaken to the progenitor of all life, death, and dreams: the Goddess. Abandoning this source requires a denial of its existence. This denial allows the "self" to escape suffering, but such a denial requires "cultivating," in that a great deal of effort on the part of the self is required to nurture and foster this renunciation. This is quite thorny in that it necessitates the rejection of a permanent, unchanging self—hence, it precludes any atonement with the "permanent, unchanging" source of the Noble Truth, the Goddess silence which rounds the waking, dreaming, and dreamless states of AUM. As the Dalai Lama admits, the rejection of an unchanging self is, and has been since the beginnings of Buddhist thought, quite "problematic":

> In this context, the notion of the self becomes crucial. The person who is experiencing suffering is oneself, and the one who needs to apply the means to dispel suffering is also oneself. And

the cause for this is within oneself. When Buddhism first appeared in ancient India, a fundamental distinction between Buddhist versus non-Buddhist views concerned the self. Specifically, the Buddhists refuted the existence of a permanent, unchanging self. Why? Because the very notion of an unchanging self, when applied to the self as an agent and to the self as the experiencer, is very problematic. From the very beginning, there was a great deal of thought and discussion concerning the nature of the self.[231]

It appears that, in order to deny and thereby escape suffering, the self must reject any potentiality of existence upon attainment of *nirvana*, for atonement with any unchanging source, be it "self" or any concept of an "all-inclusive other," is a continuation of being which negates the extinguishment of self and the subsequent cessation of suffering. "If all life is sorrowful," then escaping the suffering of sorrow is to escape any form of existence, including the "unchanging self." Then, how does the Buddha, in the form of himself, return from *nirvana* to teach his doctrine?

In modern times, such an attempt to rectify the unintelligible desire of the self to escape from "self" can be readily discerned in the work of Sigmund Freud. The Buddhist concept of escaping suffering to extinguish one's self can be recognized through equating it to Sigmund Freud's Nirvana Principle. Accepting the notion that "life is painful," Freud posited the existence of a "death wish." The Nirvana Principle identifies a need in the uneasy psyche, a wish or innate drive, for the reestablishment of a stasis state to end "the slings and arrows of outrageous fortune," and hence one's suffering. Freud called this death wish "Thanatos," in reference to the Greek mythological demon, who personified death itself. In essence, Thanatos is concerned with the preservation of the self from suffering; as such, it is complementary to Eros, the principle devoted to the propagation of life and its inherent suffering.

Ultimately, however, as Hamlet realizes, when it comes to escaping the enigmatic nature of tormented life, there is "a rub": One may avoid suffering through extinguishment, but by so doing, one will never live "at one" with the ecstatic rapture of eternal bliss. The extinguishment of self is a denial of the drive or wish for unending life, Eros, also inherent in the psyche. After all, Thanatos and Eros are complements of a Gestalt whole "more than the sum of its parts." Thus, desiring the extinguishment of the self (Thanatos) is as much an inane surrendering to temptation as is succumbing to the temptations of fear and desire (Eros), which the Buddha rejects. Consequently, whether one embraces Thanatos or Eros is inconsequential—for they are one and the same, identical temptations—the giving into which is equally self-serving. In essence, the Buddha out of fear also succumbs to temptation—in this case, to the desire for extinguishment—and ultimately to the tragic loss of one's dreams.

Native American

As the familiar axiom suggests, "There is an exception to every rule"; however, especially true for the purpose of this study, it is this "exception that proves the rule," in that Native American mythologies do not oppose the nature affirming awakenings of our prehistoric ancestors; rather, they embrace them. In contrast, for example, to the denial of a perpetual self or to a fall from Eden, living "at one" with nature can be ubiquitously recognized among the various Native American tribal peoples, as evidenced by their faith in the spiritual healing potentialities of dreams and mythologies and the "interconnectivity" of all creation. Roxanne Struthers interviewed Ojibwa and Cree women healers and here reiterates their belief in the atonement of humanity with all the web of life:

> We are all related to all living things, beings, and people. There is oneness in the universe, and all thoughts and actions influence others. When interconnected, other worlds exist and our spirit can soar and travel to the stars, other plains, and under the earth. Also, connection with nature is paramount, as knowledge of self

comes from nature. This oneness is foundational in the component of spirituality, which is defined as interconnectedness with self, others, nature, and God/ Life Force/ Absolute / Transcendent…in holistic practice.[232]

Importantly, Struthers identifies the cultural and spiritual sources of the healing wisdom of these women, especially noting the important role of visions and dreams: "All of the research participants felt their indigenous culture was subdued and oppressed by the dominant culture. Each woman learned about her culture, values, and traditions in diverse manners. They obtained this knowledge from people who raised them, a person encountered on their life journey, genetic memory contained with their indigenous being, dreams or visions, or a combination of these modes."[233]

Dreams and visions, most notably those achieved through "vision quests," are popularly recognized Native American sources of spiritual healing. Unfortunately, however, as evidenced by misinformed movie productions and the current over commercialization of "dreamcatchers" by non-Native American retailers, the importance of dreams as vehicles of spiritual healing for indigenous peoples has been devalued and misunderstood. As a result, it has now become necessary to restore their more potent meanings. Dreamcatchers, for example, have become mostly ornamental novelties in American society today; however, among Native American tribes, most notably the Ojibwa, dreamcatchers were utilitarian—designed to protect sleepers from nightmares generated by evil spirits.

The Ojibwa word for dreamcatcher is *assbikeshinh* (phonetic spelling), which refers to spiders. This comparison is due to the web-like structure of the dreamcatcher but also for its allusion to the protective, mythological Earth-Mother, Spider Old Woman.[234] As such, they were prophylactic in nature and hung over beds, especially the bedding of children, to protect them as they slept from the invasion of bad dreams and thoughts. To achieve this, a dreamcatcher is constructed by stringing loosely woven netting inside the frame of a wooden hoop, which is then adorned with feathers and beads—but not simply for their decorative value. Rather, the belief is that during the night, bad dreams would be trapped in the netting, but good dreams would be able to slide down the feathers to the dreamer. The morning light would then evaporate the bad dreams and thoughts trapped in the webbing into nothingness.

In much the same way, Native American vision quests are also too often misunderstood in popular culture. Though both vision quests and dreams were communications with sacred sources, vision quests differed in that they were "individually initiated":

> Deeper knowledge than what had been originally allotted to human beings was possible only if the spirits, through the mediation of other creatures, shared some of their knowledge with us. Thus there came about a ritual in which humans set aside time from their routine lives and opened themselves up to the possibility of establishing relationships with spirits and other creatures. This ritual was the vision quest, a time and means for seeking communications from nonhuman sources. The vision quest differs from dreams or daytime sacred events in that it is almost wholly dependent on the initiative of the human, whereas the other two means of establishing a relationship occur because of the initiative of higher powers.[235]

Nevertheless, this said, Deloria admits that the decision to undertake most vision quests was usually initiated by "dreams in which they were instructed to make themselves available."[236] Thus, dreams and/or the hearing of voices were often calls to spiritual adventure, reminiscent of Joseph Campbell's call of the "hero with a thousand faces" as the first step of one's mythological journey to receive the boons of spiritual powers and bring them back to the benefit of one's society.

As an example of the mythological nature of dreams, Campbell relates the vision of Black Elk, an Oglala Lakota Sioux medicine man. When Black Elk was a young boy of around nine years old, he became very sick, especially psychologically so. Under this hypnogogic state, he experienced a prophetic vision of the disasters his tribe would soon be facing from their encounters with the American cavalry. In his dream, he saw that the "hoop" of his nation was just one of many such hoops, and all the hoops of his nation worked together, cooperating in "grand procession." Here, Campbell reveals Black Elk's epiphany and discusses its mythopoeic importance:

> But more than that, the vision was an experience of himself as going through the realms of spiritual imagery that were of his culture and assimilating their import. It comes to one great statement, which for me is a key statement to the understanding of myth and symbols. He says, "I saw myself on the central mountain of the world, the highest place, and I had a vision because I was seeing in the sacred manner of the world." And the sacred central mountain was Harney Peak in South Dakota. And then he says, "But the central mountain is everywhere."
>
> That is a real mythological realization. It distinguishes between the local cult image, Harney Peak, and its connotation as the center of the world. The center of the world is the *axis mundi,* the central point, the pole around which all revolves. The central point of the world is the point where stillness and movement are together. Movement is time, but stillness is eternity. Realizing how this moment of your life is actually a moment of eternity, and experiencing the eternal aspect of what you're doing in the temporal experience—this is the mythological experience.[237]

This prophetic experience of Black Elk, brought about by his impaired sense of wakefulness—equivalent to the altered state of consciousness experienced due to the deprivation of food and drink during vision quests—illustrates another strong connection between dreams and vision quests, in that dreams can also have stages of "twilight"[238] as one crosses the boundary between dream and waking consciousness: hypnogogic and hypnopompic states. Succinctly, hypnogogic episodes can occur as one drowsily gets overcome by sleep; in contrast, hypnopompic episodes can occur as one tries to awaken. Both states can cause auditory and visual hallucinations similar to those reported by vision questers, including the hearing of voices to which Deloria alludes. Additionally, hypnopompic episodes can also be accompanied by convincing olfactory hallucinations. Furthermore, like vision quests, dreams—through the practice of lucid dreaming—can also be individually initiated and controlled, thereby enforcing their identification. In essence, regardless of the perceived source of initiation, both dreams and vision quests are communications with higher spiritual powers in order to establish healing relationships—to the benefit of the individual and/or, as in mythological hero quests, one's society.

Because Native Americans place such great value on the interconnectivity of all life, shared dreams are especially perceived to be omens, portending good or evil, from spiritual beings. Deloria relates an incident involving Luther Standing Bear who, at the time of the dream, was recruiting Native Americans for one of Buffalo Bill's Wild West tours. Standing Bear's uncle Wakan Hunska, frightened by a dream, warned him not to embark on his train journey to join the show, but Standing Bear had already committed to do so and continued his preparations, disregarding the old man's dream. But to his surprise, on the morning of the journey, Standing Bear was approached by two young men who asked him to find replacements for them, as both had simultaneously dreamt of disaster. The night before, both had been jolted awake by the deafening sound of a crash and the screams of frightened people. Disregarding the warnings once again, Standing Bear boarded the train with his entourage. Just outside of Chicago, their train was hit by a speeding train. The passenger car Standing Bear and a number of other Lakota braves were riding in was destroyed, and dead bodies were violently strewn among the rubble of splintered steel. Standing Bear survived despite being severely injured. When he saw Wakan Hunska once again, his uncle scolded him, for that which he had dreamt had come to pass. Deloria concludes by affirming the sacred connection of dreams and higher spiritual powers: "This account I believe stands between the power dream and the real-life situations of the sacred that have great clarity and are easily identified as the initiative of the sacred spiritual powers."[239]

The Native American belief in the interconnectivity of all humanity and all life redresses the destructive dissociation of self and other, which isolates one from the spirit that informs and instructs all existence. Through dreams, one communicates with the very essence of one's soul, allowing the "self" to atone with "selflessness," the experience of which awakens one to wholeness, holiness, and health.

Contemporary Spiritual Dream Healing

It is important here to differentiate between spiritual healing and the numerous manifestations of paranormal dreaming—for example telepathy, out of body experiences (including alien abductions), and clairvoyant dreams—because although paranormal dreams are often reported, there is no definitive research to support claims of their legitimacy. This is not to say, however, that such a preternatural connection does not exist. For example, in a renowned study, Montague Ullman devised an experiment utilizing a "sender," "monitor," and "receiver" to test the telepathic nature of dreams. Succinctly, the sender and receiver were monitored on EEGs. Whenever the sender began REM sleep, he or she was awakened by the observer and was told to send an image to the receiver during his or her REM sleep. Over the six year course of his studies, Ullman recorded an impressive 75% success rate of telepathic transmission.

In fact, the occurrence of *psi* dreaming is so pervasive that most of the students in my "Interpretation of Dreams" courses or who attend my lectures cite their experiences of telepathic and precognitive dreaming as the main reason they participated, as for instance this type of dream: Ms. X is an Asian exchange student, currently studying in the United States. Just recently, she became engaged to one of her classmates, who is not Asian. She told the group that during a very troubling dream, she saw herself walking down the aisle at her wedding. She heard a gunshot and realized that someone was trying to kill her. Upon waking, she telephoned her mother to tell her about the dream. To her horror, her mother excitedly exclaimed that Ms. X's father was on his way to America to stop her wedding, and in his anger, he proclaimed that if he had to, he would shoot her.

Perhaps, in one of the most famous examples of precognitive dreaming, President Lincoln dreamt about his own death. He saw a crowd of people sobbing and crying around a coffin. He asked, "Who died?" A soldier responded that it was the President, and that he had been killed by an assassin. This dream occurred only a few days before Lincoln's assassination. Nevertheless, however intriguing these paranormal incidences may be, for the purpose of this study, the question remains: Do dreams positively affect spiritual health?

Indeed, they do. Dreams that are "sacred" are tied to positive adjustment. Research conducted by Phillips and Pargament draws a solid connection between sanctification of dreams and healing: " …[I]t was found that the more sacred the dream was perceived, the more beneficial the outcome reported from a stressful life event which related to the dream. These outcomes include less negative affect and more positive affect, psychological and spiritual growth."[240]

Though spiritual dreaming is rare, when it does occur, it appears to have genuine curative value. As Phillips and Pargament found:

Sanctification of dreams was related to positive outcomes, not to negative outcomes. That is, individuals who viewed the dream as a manifestation of God or as having sacred qualities reported higher levels of stress-related growth, spiritual growth, and positive affect towards the stressful life event they believed most related to the dream…. Overall, the results suggest that sanctifying a dream can have positive implications for adjustment to a stressful life event that is linked to the dream.[241]

Kuiken, Lee, Eng, and Singh also report a correlation between transcendent dreams and a subsequent spiritual transformation, specifically an awakening to interconnectivity: " …[T]he type of spiritual transformation associated with transcendent dreams involved an ecstatic sense of release from everyday entanglements…. [A]nd transcendent dreams moved the dreamer toward an unbounded sense of life, in all things."[242]

In Dancing Between Worlds: Jung and the Native American Soul, Fred R. Gustafson, a strong proponent of Native American culture and the spiritual healing of dreams as interpreted through a Jungian psychoanalytical perspective, cites one of his dreams as an illustrative awakening to interconnectivity. In his dream, the pleasant atmosphere of a weekend retreat is threatened by the appearance of a man who kept entrapping him in philosophical discussion about the contrasts between people and the natural world. But Gustafson, sure of himself, pointed to a tree outside the window and asked the man if it were alive. He answered, "Yes." Gustafson asked the man if he were alive, and, if alive, did he have a soul? Again he said, "Yes." Then Gustafson said, "If you are alive and, because of this, have a soul, and the tree is alive, does it not mean that the tree has a soul also?" He said, "I guess a little bit." Gustafson replied, "That 'little bit' is what you must now think on."[243] Here, Gustafson interprets the spiritual message of his dream:

This dream reflects the struggle of most people in general today. The debate in the dream challenges the notion that humankind is not part of the natural order of things and, conversely, the natural order does not include humankind. Such a view separates us from the ecosystem, viewing it as one would an aquarium from the outside rather than seeing ourselves as vitally linked to it. If we go wrong, it goes wrong and vice versa. Jung states, "Without soul, spirit is dead as matter, because both are artificial abstractions; whereas man originally regarded spirit as a volatile body, and matter is not lacking in soul."[244]

As the rising levels of addiction, poverty, senseless violence, and disregard for the value of human life in today's society demonstrate, contemporary culture is losing any recognition of "soul in matter."[245] Hence, dreams are becoming more and more essential to redressing this loss of spirit which isolates, degrades, and dehumanizes the individual. Therefore, Phillips and Pargament recommend a clinical awakening to the benefits of spiritual dreaming: "…[D]reams that are perceived as sacred are tied to positive adjustment. Clinicians should be aware of these beneficial relationships, and be prepared to incorporate significant, memorable dreams as potential aids to adjustment."[246] As they conclude:

Such dreams can elucidate a sense of spiritual connection. Pargament (1997) has described how one's relationship with a higher power can aid the coping process. Feeling a sense of connection and support from the divine can aid in dealing with stressful life events.

In summary, clinicians can explore whether dreams are viewed as holy and sacred, manifestations of God and what this means to the client. By exploring how the dream might be beneficial, new ways of viewing or acting towards a stressful life event might be elicited that further adjustment to the event and growth. In conclusion, this research highlights the need for psychologists to return to the "early days of the field," when dreams were considered to play a significant role in adapting to life's demands.[247]

Just as spiritual dreams help us to deal with life, they can also help us to understand the tragedy of our mortality—the death of our loved ones and of ourselves. Dreaming of someone who has died can be an expression of grief, yet most of these dreams are more reassuring than upsetting, perhaps because they demonstrate a kind of interconnectivity of spirit and even place. For example, when my father passed away from a devastating illness, I dreamt that he was young and healthy again and living in Manhattan with his new family. When I awoke, I was puzzled but relieved. It was calming to think that, perhaps, there was life after death and to feel that he was all right. I realize, of course, that this dream was also a healing stage in my grieving process, one which was telling me that it would be best for me to keep living rather than to concentrate on death—it was time to "let go" and "move on."

In this sense, spiritual dreams are like prayers, in that they seem to be a form of afterlife. However, they differ in that prayers bridge the unconscious with waking consciousness; whereas, dreams link us to the very source from where all deity arises. As a result, dreams function as communications both from God and to God. Such a connection can elucidate a sense of spiritual wellbeing, which can help us cope with stressful life events as well as with our mortality. Illness and tragedy disrupt our personal narratives. Dreams help us to remedy this loss by creating new narratives and building a sense of spirituality; they bring the concepts of grace and holiness into the areas of our lives that need healing, so that we can recreate ourselves and awaken to a new narrative, one of "wholeness" of self-identity—open to health and mending. They are like hidden "wormholes" in mystical spiritual space, portals allowing us to transcend the confines of an ailing self to resurrection as a new healthy being.

Consequently, although it is important that dream researchers specialize in their respective fields, it is more important, however, to recognize that truly comprehending dreams can only be achieved through an interdisciplinary process that creates a "whole more than the sum of its parts." Thus, neurophysicists, psychoanalysis, and spiritualists must explore each element of the tripartite elements of dreams—physical, mental, and spiritual—to ensure a quality of understanding. But the second, and more crucial step, of the analytical process is to recognize how the pieces "work together" to awaken us to the hidden messages, the very themes, of our mortal and immortal selves. Ultimately, this interdisciplinary perspective, at the heart of the medical humanities, redresses the myopic "blindness" in any field of isolated research and figuratively creates the spiritual "third-eye" to complete the physical and mental perceptions. For in dreams, matter, mind, and spirit become one.

In this, the tripartite nature of dreams to positively affect physical, mental, and spiritual health can be seen to parallel yet transcend the triune composition of atoms,[248] the building blocks of matter. Actually, atoms are themselves built of subatomic particles like gluons and quarks and what has been deemed "the God particle." In a sense, they are like Russian babushka nesting dolls, wherein a new organism is found to be at the core of the one enclosing it—and on and on like "riddles wrapped in enigmas inside mysteries."[249] As a result, they eventually prove to be hollow, vacuous, in that there is nothing in the last one. Therefore, searching for any God particle in subatomic fields is fruitless because it is a process reminiscent of peeling an onion or dissecting a seed. One can never detect the unknown "creator" at the core—that which builds the onion or awakens the seed to blossom.

In contrast, dreams reside in the hollow, the vacuum, and take us to that which informs us all. Dreams have no matter, yet they are all matter. They are all that matters. They are the psychopompoi, the guides to our souls. So if any "true" God particle is to ever to be found, it will be discovered in our dreams. Pursuing our dreams will never prove fruitless, for in essence, dreams—"chief nourishers in life's feast"—are the sweetest fruits of life; without them, existence would be very bitter, indeed.

Chapter Four

DREAMS AND PHYSICAL HEALTH

Though fascination with dreams is one of the earliest of human preoccupations, it is among the youngest of applied sciences. Arguably, it was not until Hans Berger recorded the first electroencephalogram (EEG) in 1924 that neuroscientists could seriously begin to investigate the so-called "secrets" of dreams: Do they possess any intelligible meaning? Do they serve any therapeutic purpose? Today, thanks to technological advances in cellular neuromodulator recording and Positron Emission Tomographic (PET) imaging, contemporary neuroscientists, excavating the darkness of night's mysteries, are unearthing amazing revelations about the importance of dreaming to the maintenance of physical health and wellbeing.

When one's life is disrupted by illness, one's life story or "narrative" is broken. Succinctly, dreams rewrite life narratives in an effort to redress or restore the healing needed to continue living productively. Like journal writing and the keeping of diaries, dreams help us formulate strategies to deal with our broken life stories by "tapping into" the unconscious as conduit to a wealth of occult wisdom—beyond reason—that is not accessible to sensory limited waking states of consciousness. As importantly, dreams connect us to the "language of our bodies"; that is, through the "pillow talk" of dreams, our bodies "speak" to us and awaken us to the importance of the body-mind relationship as well as to the healing potentialities of restoring the self to some sense of "wholeness."

Unfortunately, however, the body-mind continuum inherent in dream structures often goes unrecognized or misunderstood. As

Meredith Sabini explains: "But perhaps we don't recognize 'somatic dreams' because the symbol system that the dreaming mind uses to portray the vegetative and organic aspects of our existence has not yet been worked out. We are pretty good at elucidating the metaphors of our psychological selves in dreams, but the biological, interpersonal, and cultural dimensions of dreaming have received significantly less study."[250]

At the Tavistock Lectures (London 1935), presented to a medical audience, Carl Gustav Jung also identified the physiological communications of dreams: "Because of the possible unity of the two things, we must expect to find dreams which are more on the physiological side than the psychological, as we have other dreams that are more on the psychological than the physical side."[251] Sabini cites the work of Fordham, who also recognized this harmony of soma and psyche as complements of one "unity": "British analyst Michael Fordham viewed psyche and soma as two aspects of one unity: 'if we follow the idea of the psyche being at all points related to physical processes, we can begin to conceive of the Self as representing a state of wholeness which includes soma and psyche.'"[252]

What the Ancients Knew

Cradles of Civilization

It is difficult to determine exactly when dreams were first used for healing purposes, but most experts would estimate about 3,000 B.C.E. or over 5,000 years ago, in the areas known as the "Cradles of Civilization." During this time, there was a great deal of interest in communicating with deities to gain what was believed to be "divine wisdom" or "knowledge"—especially through "message dreams," which were primarily verbal in nature and thought to emanate directly from the gods. Stewart Means explains the widespread importance of dreams to ancient civilizations: "…[Dreams] were generally regarded as one of the means chosen by the gods to reveal themselves or their wishes to men. The reality of these visions or revelations was seldom if ever doubted. As a consequence, from the very earliest antiquity the influence of dreams is one of the outstanding facts which is universally recognized. Every people and every literature show the presence of this fact."[253]

Means concludes by stressing the healing nature of dreams:

It was generally considered that dreams were not only one of the most natural but one of the most important means of communication between gods and men, or between the unseen world and its inhabitants and those who are still upon earth. It was through dreams also that the healing power of the gods was used, and many sick visited the temples of Aesculapius and other gods of healing in order to be recovered of their sickness. This was not mere ignorant superstition of the stolid mass, but was held as a fact which could be proven by unquestionable testimony in the most enlightened age of the Roman Empire. Pliny, Galen the great physician, Marcus Aurelius the noblest spirit of his age, all these as well as others were firmly convinced that dreams had a magical power to restore health and banish disease.[254]

Some of the earliest evidence of ancient "message" dreams dating to the near beginnings of recorded history has been discovered on cuneiform tablets. According to Harry A. Hoffner:

Cuneiform tablets record that such [message] dreams were reported through royal officials to Zimrilim, the King of Mari (1779-1761 B.C.), Sin-kashid of Uruk, and Ashurbanipal of Assyria (668-631). It is possible also that the messages from Ishtar of Arbela and from Bel to Esarhaddon and the king's mother, which were delivered to royal officials by various private citizens (mostly women) who were apparently not professional prophets, were dreams.[255]

More specifically, for example, is the dream of Hittite crown prince Muwatalli concerning the health of his brother: " Such a dream came to Muwatalli, the Hittite crown prince, regarding the health of his younger brother Hattusili III. Muwatalli reported the dream to his father Mursili, much as the commoners at Mari reported theirs to the royal officials. In the dream the goddess Shaushka predicted that young Hattusili would die unless his father dedicated him immediately to her as a priest."[256]

However, most dreams are not verbal messages; therefore, they required the expertise of seers or prophets for interpretation, as illustrated by one of Mursili II's dreams, which demonstrates the all-important healing potentialities of body-mind relationships. Mursili dreamt that a deity touched his mouth in judgmental fashion: "Eventually this dream produced a severe psychological trauma, manifesting itself in hysterical aphonia (or aphasia), which persisted for some time and was the occasion for an elaborate healing ritual."[257]

Such healing rituals often focused on dream incubation, through which the content of dreams could be controlled to redress health issues. The goddess Gula, "the great healer," was particularly associated with incubation dreams, as it was believed that she appeared in dream visions "to make whole again those things that were broken."

Similarly in Egypt, temples to the "god of healing," Imhotep, were renowned for dream incubation practices:

Incubation is the term historically used to describe a variety of practices, carried out before sleep, aimed at causing a person to dream about a particular topic. The incubation of dreams was a popular and elaborately developed art in Egypt from early times well into the Roman era. The "Masters of the Secret Things" practiced their rituals and interpretations at special temples to which people would come to incubate dreams. The temple at Memphis, dedicated to Imhotep, the god of healing, was the most important of the-se.[258]

This is not to say, however, that unsolicited dreams were not also prognosticators of medical conditions and guides of therapeutic treatment. Such dreams often provided spontaneous "breakthroughs" for potential healing methodologies: "What are classed as unsolicited dreams are those cases where revelation was given by a dream of the hiding-place of some wonderful chapter for use in funerary or medicinal magic, such as the traditional origin of formulae in the "Books of the Dead," and the first medical papyri."[259] Nevertheless, these were rarer incidences, as the popularity of the dream temple sanctuaries demonstrates. Pilgrims eagerly sought-out both incubation procedures and priestly medical wisdom to invite dreams, for example:

> Solicited dreams were more frequent. The Kings when in a difficult situation would implore the Gods for guidance. They would go to a temple, and after prayer and sleep, a dream would answer their wishes. Cures were also obtained in this way. The story of Satui tells of Mahituaskhit going to the temple of Imuthes in Memphis, praying, falling asleep and receiving from the God in a dream a cure for her sterility.[260]

Arguably, in fact, the roots of modern day hypnosis can be attributed to ancient Egyptian Dream Temples, where "suggestion therapy" was utilized over 4000 years ago to heal patients' medical conditions—probably in a similar way to how placebos work today, through suggestion. By interpreting these induced dreams, the temple seers and prophets could form diagnoses and fashion treatment therapies. Such openness to the hypnotic suggestion inherent in dream incubation temples may actually have a physiological root in our very DNA. James McClenon explains:

> Hominids are assumed to have devised more complex rituals, producing therapeutic altered states of consciousness (ASC). At some stage, *Homo Sapiens* devised shamanic/hypnotic therapies, coupling ASC with suggestion. Because such practices were effective, these rituals selected for genotypes associated with hypnotizability. With increased

frequency of these genotypes, religious sentiment, myths [and hence dreams], and ideologies justifying ritual became possible.

Genetic research provides evidence supporting this scenario. Religious sentiment (the attitudes, thoughts, and judgments prompted by feelings associated with therapeutic ASC) has a genetic basis.[261]

Interestingly, in Egypt, such dream incubation suggestions were also used to help the dead and dying navigate their journeys from waking life to the afterlife. Illustrative of Hamlet's fear of the eternal nightmares that may perpetually haunt the afterlife, death is a nightmarish existence wrought with peril and not an escape from the "slings and arrows" of waking—the Egyptian afterlife was an awakening[262] to another potentially of life.

For in that sleep of death what dreams may come,
When we have shuffled off this mortal coil,
Must give us pause (3.1.67-69).[263]

As Ogden Goelet asserts:

...[O]rder and disorder continued to exist side by side both in this world and beyond it. If the *Book of the Dead* often appears surreal and confusing, let us remember that it describes what happens after death, the moment when one left the orderly world of Egypt and confronted nonexistence and chaos. The notion that the next world might be perilous, confusing, and predictable is hardly unique to Egyptian culture, but the Egyptians universalized the irrationality: not only mortals but the gods themselves had to contend with the same perils.[264]

Consequently, incubation was essential to prepare and guide individuals as they navigated the perilous waters of death and dreams. Through *kataskeue*, or "preparation," the dreamer or supplicant is readied to accept divine revelations, for the use of suggestion can be perceived to have been an identical process for incubating dreams and death—the former to affect healing in waking life and the latter to affect the healing of one's heart so purified in death that it would be judged "lighter than a feather" before Osiris.

This need for protective incubation can be illustrated by the goddess Isis herself, who embodies the life/death dichotomy inherent in divine dream messages. She was identified with healing and the healing arts; she is the mother of Horus and life-restorer of her dismembered husband Osiris. However, she was also the slayer of the sun god Ra and architect of her brother Seth's ignominious defeat. As such, she demonstrates the simultaneous powers to give life, to restore it, and to take it away. Alluding to the arcane "Isis to Horus" text, Jeffrey B. Pettis explains:

> The process of *kataskeue'* yields the secrets of re-generation. This entails a bringing to consciousness the deeper regions and images within the initiate (and the one engaged in the text). These become themselves the material of metamorphoses and/or healing.
>
> Becoming aware—obtaining knowledge—appears to have a positive value in the Isis to Horus story. Elixirs may have the potential to heal or poison. Dreams may heal and/or madden.[265]

Greco-Roman Era

Succeeding the Egyptian era, during the Greek and Roman ascendancies, dream incubation was also used to prepare patients so that, with the proper suggestions from priests, they could receive healing messages from the gods. Incubation temples, most notably the over 400 sanctuaries dedicated to Asclepius, were the most popular. Here Gayle Delaney recreates what might have been a typical patient's temple experience:

> …[I]magine that you are ill and have journeyed to the Askleopion at Epidaurus. You have walked on the *via sacra* for five miles from the port into a place of exquisite beauty. As you approach the entrance, you read on the stone stelae the

inscriptions of the famous cures Asclepius has granted to other pilgrims. Harmless snakes, symbols of the god, move about freely. You enter the sacred precinct, bathe, and perform purification rituals and preliminary sacrifices before going to sleep in a special place in the temple. If Asclepius appears as himself or as a dog or a snake in a dream or vision, you will be cured. You can stay at Epidaurus for as long as it takes to have the necessary dream. Finally Asclepius appears in your dream and touches the sick part of your body and disappears. If the tradition holds true, you awaken healed, pay fees to the priests, and make offerings of thanks. From now on you will have a deep belief in the god of your dream, and this just might help prolong the effects of your cure.[266]

Importantly to this study, in these havens, the medical profession recognized the fundamental discovery of the healing potentialities of physically generated dreams. As a result, ancient Greek medical writers differentiated between divinely-inspired dreams and those that were more "natural" and "true." Lee Pearcy asserts, " ...[T]hey [the ancient medical writers] were interested in the dreams that were both natural and true, from which a physician could gain information about bodily states and processes that were hidden from direct observation."[267]

Specifically, as an example, Cilliers and Retief cite the significance of the *On Dreams* (*Regimen* 4) text:
While it was from earliest times commonly accepted that dreams have a divine origin and that certain dreams entail messages from the gods to individuals, the author of the Hippocratic treatise *On Dreams (Regimen 4)* was arguably the first Greek to distinguish between prophetic dreams sent by the gods and dreams with a purely physical origin which could have a prognostic and diagnostic purpose. In the sanctuaries of Asclepius, these two kinds of dreams have in a way merged, being a message from the god on medical matters. The core of the treatment in these Asclepieia was the incubation or

enkoimesis, during which the patients hoped to experience a dream visit from the god who would cure them directly or otherwise give advice on medicaments or treatment.[268]

Additionally, a circa fifth century Hippocratic treatise, *On Regimen*, is equally interesting because of its exploration of the "causes" of dreams. As such:

> ...*On Regimen* is anomalous in the literature of ancient medicine. Most medical writers and schools, with the prominent exception of Galen, did not concern themselves with the aetiology or mechanism of dreams. Instead, they used dreams as a diagnostic and prognostic tool without committing themselves to any explanation of how or why dreams reflected physiological reality. It was enough to accept that a patient's dreams might be part of the ensemble of information that the physician brought to bear in his attempt to construct an account of the patient's condition, and an appropriate therapy for it.[269]

Similarly, Artemidorus' *Oneirocritica,*[270] as Christine Walde suggests, also "seems to open a window to the ancient world." Here, she explains the importance of dream interpretation to the 2nd century C.E. medical profession:

> Since illness, like dreams, is something that all people experience, either personally or by witnessing how it affects someone else, it naturally appears in the imagery and interpretations of the *Oneirocritica*. Moreover, as the body and its wellbeing were the most important economic resource for everybody, especially for the poor and destitute, we may assume that the loss of health and consequently of self-sustenance must have been a constant fear and preoccupation. Indeed, in the veritable *Totentanz* of the *Oneirocritica,* fragility and finality, illness and death are lurking around every corner.[271]

Artemidorous discussed the difference between the dreams of sick persons and healthy individuals' precognitive dreams. Regarding ill patients' dreams, Walde explains: "The interpretation focuses not on the outbreak but on the course of illness, including therapy, surgery, deterioration, cure and death.... [B]ut the dream image is not exclusively interpreted in terms of his [the patient's] own illness.... According to this grid—in anticipation of the Freudian condensation—an image might have more than one meaning."[272]

Whereas, in regards to dreams that predict impending illness, Artemidorous differentiates between those that portend ill health for the dreamer and, interestingly, those that warn of impending sickness for someone else. Furthermore, these dreams predicting impending health problems can themselves be divided into two types:

> [i] dreams that predict illness of the dreamer *and* the course of illness; if the dream is "personal," this means a dream image concerning the dreamer alone; and (ii) dreams of a healthy person which predict illness/death for someone else, that is, for a different person, if it is an "alien" dream.... Even if there are a few vicarious dreams among the incubations dreams...the fact that one can have dreams about somebody else's disease/health is certainly the most prominent difference to medical dream interpretation.[273]

Walde concludes that for Artemidorous, the "morally tainted" associations contemporary culture applies to illness, for example, to AIDS, did not exist. "For Artemidorus, illness has no special metaphors—it is neither a taboo nor is it demonized. It is one of those conditions of bad luck human beings have to come to terms with."[274]

So how did ancient dream healers help patients "come to terms with" illness? In "Earth, Dream, and Healing: The Integration of *Materia* and Psyche in the Ancient World," Jeffrey Pettis posits that Asclepius cults used a variety of herbs and minerals as medicinal applications. Numerous texts and treatises outlined and cataloged the uses and dangers of these treatments, for example the works of Pliny the Elder's (23-79 C.E.) highly organized scientific analysis of plants, and

Theophrastus' (370-287 B.C.E.) work regarding the cultivation, medicinal applications, and hazards of using vegetal types: "Theophrastus, successor of Aristotle at the Lyceum, sets out a systematic cataloguing and discussion of ancient plants and their medicinal use. In his *Inquiry into Plants* he examines 'all kinds of drugs" which include the medicinal use of fruit, extracted juice, leaves, roots, and herbs (IX, 8). He records how druggists and herb-differs harvest plants, some of which have toxic properties...."[275] A few of the medicinal treatments outlined by Pliny and Theophrastus include the use of cucumber lozenges to treat ocular afflictions; the mandrake leaf and the cyclamen root to heal and dress wounds; and utilization of erysipelas roots soaked in vinegar as a remedy for a wide range of maladies including insomnia and gout—or even as a love potion.[276]

Similarly, dream healers created medicinal unguents from such mineral sources as salt, honey and pumice:

> One Ascelpius cult testimony notes a 4th c. C.E. ungent [sic] which includes common salts, rock salts, Cappadocian salts roasted, and pumice-stone (Oribasius, *Synopsis and Eustathium* III, 162). Both Aristotle and Pliny show an extensive knowledge of minerals for medicinal purposes. Pliny's *Natural History* sets out a descriptive cataloguing of the properties of metals and stones (Bks. 33-37). He includes the identification and usage of various drugs derived from these materials. For example, when mixed with ground pumice stone, gold relieves ulcers, and "when boiled down in honey and git it acts as a gentle laxative" (33.85).[277]

Ultimately, as early writings indicate, the medicinal treatment recipes of the Asclepius dream temples appear to be derived mostly from plants and minerals. Pilgrims to the sanctuaries were induced through dream incubation suggestion to reveal the symptoms of their illnesses, from which priests as dream healers could formulate both diagnoses and treatment methodologies. In this way, the therapeutic mind-body connection was activated to awaken the dreamer to the healing potentialities inherent in the interrelatedness of humanity to all nature.

India

In a 1929 lecture to the British Royal Society of the Arts, P. Johnston-Saint illuminated the germinal role of Indian dream healers as progenitors of both modern Freudian dream interpretation as well as of the Greek, Roman, and Arabic use of herbal remedies by dream physicians. First, according to Johnston-Saint:

> In the field of what to-day we should call Psycho-Therapy the Hindus again held pride of place, and centuries before Freud was heard of, the Hindu doctors were anxiously probing into the secrets of dreams. With much that we were taught to regard till quite recently as absurd, their teaching shows signs of a good deal of our newest learning, and in for example the theories of the Terror Dream they came at least remarkably near our 20th century doctrine of the subconscious mind.[278]

Second, regarding the herbal remedies of ancient dream healers, Johnston-Saint lauds the importance of Indian *Materia Medica*, which presents an exhaustive listing of medicinal plants as outlined in their Botanical Gardening, as origin of the practice:

> This Botanical Gardening coupled with the Indian pharmaceutical gardens…seems to possess a particular interest in medical history, and again it is to India that we owe it.

> Many of these medicines can be traced directly, not only down to the Arabs but also to the Greeks and Romans. Dioscorides in his first book mentions many Indian plants particularly among aromatics for which India has always been famed. Galen and Pliny also borrowed much, but it is the work of Dioscorides that is best calculated to show to how great an extent the ancients were indebted to India and the East for their

medicines. There were some who used to think that the Hindus had their knowledge from the physicians who accompanied Alexander the Great on his conquests in the East, but we now know that it was to India that the Greeks, and so indirectly ourselves, owe most of their medicines.[279]

As Johnston-Saint declares, "To-day the speculation is over and we trace how the great Pythagoras himself imbibed his mysteries from the Brahmanas of India."[280] In fact, there is ample evidence, supported by findings from Northwestern Indian excavations, to conclude that as early as 3000 B.C.E., dream healers from Babylonia, Egypt, Ceylon, Java and even China and Tibet were instructed by Indian physicians.[281]

Similarly, the first classification of dreams also appears to be rooted in pre-current epoch Indian medical lore. Briefly, in ancient India, dreams were categorized by two classes, as either auspicious or inauspicious: " The simplest division is into auspicious (*subha*) and inauspicious (*asubha*). The division is seen to be very ancient by the words *svapna* and *duhsvapna* to mean good and bad dreams...."[282] Simply, auspicious dreams have desirable effects, while conversely inauspicious dreams lead to undesirable effects.

The Jaina *Ristasamuccaya* further divides dreams into two categories: those told by a god and those that occur "naturally":
...[D]ream is twofold. One is that which is told by the god and the other is a natural dream. That dream is a dream told by a god where a *mantra* (sacred formula) is recited.
...[T]he other (viz., a natural dream) occurs when one, void of worries and well-poised body and well-proportioned humours, gets [it], indeed, without (muttering) a *mantra* (sacred formula).[283]

This recognition of the need to balance "humors," which later gained prominence in Western medical practices, demonstrates how ancient Indian healers used dreams to identify imbalances of temperaments to diagnose illness. More specifically, referencing the "void" of "well-proportioned humours" revealed through natural dreams in the *Ristasamuccaya*, Wayman illustrates how the over-prominence of each humor could be recognized in dreams:

> The expression "lacking well-proportioned humours" suggests the threefold division where pathological disorders are explained in the medical works to involve imbalance of the three humours, "wind," "bile," and "phlegm." In the sixty-eighth Parisista of the *Atharva-Veda* men are said to have the temperaments bilious (fiery), phlegmatic (watery), and sanguine (windy). Different dreams are attributed to such persons respectively: for the bilious, dreams, for example of arid land and of burning objects; for the phlegmatic, dreams, for example, of nature in splendor and burgeoning life; for the sanguine, dreams, for example of racing clouds and of forest creatures running in terror.[284]

The birth of Buddhist thought in India allowed for dreams to be reinterpreted as the brain's "sixth sense." All five concrete senses are specialized; the ear, for example, is built to transmit sounds, and the eyes are created for the purpose of sight. In like manner, the brain has a sixth "subtle" sense organ, specialized to receive communications from that occult source which is not able to be detected by the other senses; this "sense" is specialized to transmit dreams to the brain. As a result, dreams are perceived by the mind to be subtle "objects" that cannot be understood by any of the other sensory organs.

Therefore, when it retires into itself in sleep, the dream is its own object, hence a *presentation* of that perception alone, to which the five external sense organs cannot contribute. Bhavaviveka [sixth century C.E. founder of *Svatantrika,* a syllogistic approach to Buddhism, which allows for assertions] explains that the perception that is based on the sixth-sense mind (*manovijnana*) and that has the *dharmas* ("mentals" or "natures") as object is what perceives the dream. Hence this *manovijnana* is equivalent to Kashmere Saivism's *buddhi,* conceived of as mirror-like because it not only reflects external objects as perceived through the five out senses but also displays the revived traces (*samskaras*) "at the time of free imagination, remembrance, and dream."[285]

In this sense, dream consciousness finds its base in the subtle body and, consequently, can communicate what the material senses cannot detect. Therefore, through the repetition of an incantation, one can create a controlled, incubated dream state to evoke deities, a prognostic process reminiscent of the methodologies utilized by the Greek priest-healers of the Asclepius dream temples. In India, the *Atharva-Veda*[286] declares prodromal dreams (recognized in medicinal nomenclature as possible warnings of illness or changes in health) to come from Yama, the lord of the dead, whose realm is in the south. Such dreams are not simply harbingers of death, but may suggest which analgesic treatment options should be utilized.

Caraka and Susruta both describe certain dreams as prognostics of impending disease or death. "A similar view was held by Aristotle. The Indian view is that the prophetic character of the dreams is the *adrsta* (the unseen agency), namely, the merit and demerit (*dharmadharma*) of the dreamer. Prophetic dreams (*bhavika*) did not imply a fatalistic belief, because palliative measures were indicated."[287]

In early India and, thus, the ancient world, prognostic dreams— be they communications from deities or sensory perceptions radiating from the subtle matter of our minds—were indispensable diagnostic tools and determinants of remedial medical treatment procedures.

China

Ancestor worship has always played a key role in ancient Chinese culture, especially regarding dreams as shamanic vehicles of communication with deceased loved ones—as it has throughout the globe:

> Examples of cures, charms, special medicine, and the powers of a shaman arising for the first time in dreams are found all over the world. Usually the new cure or medicine given in the dream is apt to be a variation of some existing method pertaining to the culture....
>
> In Australia cases are reported of cures and charms received in dreams. Among the Mukjarawauit one man says that his dead uncle appeared to him in sleep and taught him charms against sickness and other evils. The Chepara tribe believe that male ancestors visit sleepers and impart charms to avert evil magic.[288]

However, in China, through dreams deceased ancestors could request the enforcement of filial duties as well as provide prophecies to impact the living.

> Dream interpretation has long held importance in the culture of China, a practice perhaps encouraged by the central role of ancestor worship in Chinese society since the most ancient times. It is speculated that the ancestor worship strengthened the belief that dreams carried crucial messages necessary for performance of duties toward one's ancestors, and that through dreams the departed offered instruction in the affairs of the living.[289]

In this sense, dreams become "shamanic," in that they are vehicles through which one can commune with irrational but genuinely veracious sources of wisdom, which as Howard Giskin asserts, can become valuable prognostic tools. "Specifically, I suggest that particular elements that are preserved in some dreams in Chinese folklore are similar in structure and form to shamanic experiences as elaborated by Mircea Eliade, and that this similarly allows for an analysis of these elements as genuine representations of a type of shamanic experience...."[290]

As Giskin explains, in his essay "On the Psychology of the Unconscious," "Carl G. Jung writes that we have no right to accuse a dream of 'a deliberate maneuver calculated to deceive.' 'Nature,' Jung continues, 'is often obscure, but she is not, like man, deceitful.... The dream itself wants nothing: it is a self-evident content, a plain natural fact like the sugar in the blood of a diabetic or the fever in a patient with typhus....'"[291] Freud also believed that analyzing one's writings, including one's dreams which are themselves compositions, will lead the analyst to causes of real illness, for the dreamer is the main character, unconsciously revealing truth.

To illustrate the Chinese belief in the shamanic healing power of dreams, Giskin relates the folktale of a little girl's dream about a wish fulfilling, jeweled "seven-colored flower." After spending her day wondering about what worlds may exist beyond the horizon of the sea, she dreamt that she hid aboard a foreign ship, which took her to a magical land, where she agreed to live as the king's daughter. Soon, however, she became homesick, so the king let her go and told her to choose a gift from his secret chamber to take back with her. The seven-colored flowered jewel she chose had the power of making seven wishes come true. When the girl awoke, to her amazement, she found the flowered-jewel. After a year of wasting the wishes, the girl met a boy with no legs. She used her last wish to make him whole again, so the two could play happily together. According to Giskin: "Such dream experiences, in fact, can be of more importance than events in waking life, since in dreams persons come into face-to-face contact with powerful non-human beings ('grandfathers'), who convey 'important revelations that are the source of assistance to them in the daily round of life, and besides this, of blessings that enable them to exercise exceptional powers of various kinds....'"[292]

Giskin concludes that dreams, as in the Chinese tale of the seven-colored flower, challenge the idea that waking and dream states are separate forms of consciousness. Rather, they can be perceived to emanate from the same "imaginal" plane of being. This, in turn, suggests the possibility that, through the shamanic journeying of dreams, one can alter the realities of waking life—including the possibility of affecting improved physical as well as mental and spiritual health.

If dreams then arise from the same source as waking awareness, they take on an ontological status very similar to that of waking, and thus are a source of knowledge and experience in every way as valid as waking perception. The result is that the little girl's dream, far from being a mere fantasy or hallucination of nonexistent things, can be considered rather a reflection of an actual state of existence…. Stranger still is the possibility that this root non-physical plane may play a role in the formation of physical reality itself through volitional processes, both conscious and unconscious, thus determining what actually exists in the waking world, and hence the seemingly inexplicable carryover of the seven-colored flower into the real world of the little girl.[293]

Surprisingly and quite coincidentally, just recently I watched an episode of a Korean television series, *It's OK, This is Love,* about a neuro-psychiatrist trying to help a patient who had lost the "dream" of recovery because of the extremely horrific visual appearance of an injury. The patient was a carpenter, who accidentally amputated a portion of his hand. Although surgeons had successfully reattached the missing fingers, the very sight of the damaging wound created a loss of hope in the patient, which severely disrupted his life narrative—to the point of suicide. As an effort at remediation, the psychiatrist showed him two photos: The first was of a much less injured hand, and the second was of a far more serious hand injury than his. She then showed him photos of how each case had recovered. The lesser injured individual recovered poorly, while conversely the seriously injured person's hand healed completely. She explained to the carpenter that the physical injury was not the sole determinant of healing; rather, it was the patient's dream of faith in restoring himself to health that mattered. I believe this is what Freud and Jung and our dreams are telling us: Health comes from restoring the "wholeness" of our life narratives, be they related through folklores, myths, journals, diaries, and/or dreams.

Additionally, in the dream of the seven-colored flower, the idea that everything was simply a fanciful product of imagination is belied by the value of what one brings back to waking life through one's dreams. More specifically, in China, the girl's altruistic relinquishing of her last dream to restore the health of the little boy illustrates the ancient Chinese philosophy of self-sacrifice for the benefit of one's society. As such, this tale is also reminiscent of Joseph Campbell's belief in mythologies as illustrative of the journey of the "hero,"[294] who returns from an altered state to bestow the hard-earned boons of wisdom in service of others.

The experiences of the little girl, in fact, seem to follow those accepted as taking place in shamanic traditions throughout the world, where the otherworldly experiences of the "chosen" individual are seen to be as real as anything else that may happen to someone in waking existence; typically, the "chosen" individual is the recipient of a vision, meets a spirit guide, often in a dream, receives a magical gift that endows him or her with the power to help others, and finally in the process gains wisdom that can be used for the benefit of the wider community.[295]

However, it would be a mistake to engage solely on the Chinese metaphysical connection of dream states and waking consciousness. Although admittedly greater emphasis was placed upon emotional, affective elements, Ancient Chinese doctors were also quite pragmatic regarding the medicinal potentialities of dreams to communicate physical maladies, especially as they manifested in women, whose emotionality was perceived as receptivity to psychic connection. Therefore, in addition to their understanding of dreams as shamanistic conduits to ancestral sources of occult wisdom for the individual and society, on a more medically causal level, an early preoccupation of ancient Chinese physicians focused specifically on the sexual frustration of women and how resultant physical maladies initially revealed themselves through their dreams. As Hsiu-fen Chen asserts:

> Classical Chinese medicine provides a specific outlook and fruitful vantage point from which to explore the meaning of dreams over two millennia. Apart from non-medical views that often focused on the association of dreams with human thoughts, early Chinese medical writers significantly interpreted dreams with a more body-oriented approach, similar to how they understood and manipulated emotions corporeally. They regarded dreams as internal responses to external stimuli. From this perspective, different dream images are actually the indicators of different *qi* [more commonly recognized in the West as *chi,* defined in Oriental medicine as circulating currents of "vital energy"] functioning in certain parts of the body.[296]

Here, Hsiu-fen Chen provides an interesting example, enticingly suggestive of the early Freudian concentration on the sexual origin of the physiological impacts of hysteria[297] on women:

> For over two thousand years, Chinese doctors wrote about the connection they perceived between sexual frustration and certain illnesses in women. As early as the second century B.C.E., the famous Former Han physician Chunyu Yi recorded treating a woman surnamed Han, who was a maid in the house of King Jibei. She had fallen ill from pain in her loins and back, as well as from periodic fevers. Various doctors diagnosed her ailment as a typical case of "cold and Heat" (*hanre*). By reading her Kidney pulse, however, Chunyu suggested that her "menstrual blockage" (*yueshi bu xiz*) was due to "inner coldness" (*neihan*). He based this judgment on the sign that her "Liver pulse manifested itself as a string and over the top of the left wrist" (*ganmai xian chu zuokou*). He then asserted that it was her desire of "wanting a man yet not being able to get one" (*yu nanzi er bu ke de*) that had originally generated her ailments.

Chunyu prescribed medicinal drugs to restart her menstrual cycle and, eventually, she recovered.[298]

Due to such misperceptions by male physicians, mostly to the detriment of women, women were often stigmatized for "suffering sexual frustration and excessive desires," resulting in what doctors termed "demonic fetuses," or abnormally excessive abdominal tumescence. Hsiu-fen Chen relates one of the earliest recorded incidences of dreams as prognoses of physical ailments:

> The first medical case comes from the Yuan physician Hua Shou (ca. 134-86) who was once sent to treat the daughter of a certain temple administrator named Yang Tiancheng. According to his wife, when their daughter visited the temple at dusk, she felt her "heart touched" (*xingdong*) just at the moment when she saw a spirit-demon dressed in yellow clothes. After returning home, she began dreaming of sexual intercourse with the spirit-demon. The erotic dreams later caused belly to swell as if she were pregnant. Doctor Hua diagnosed this as a case of having a "demonic fetus" and prescribed the "decoction of peach kernel" (*taorenjian*—an abortifacient recipe)—to break the lady's abdominal congestion and blood stagnation. He recorded that the lumps of blood discharged from her body looked like tadpoles or fish eyes and that her illness was finally cured.[299]

The prodromal role of women's sexual dreams as predictors of physical illness persisted through the centuries, but was modified as early as the sixth century C.E. to include prognoses of infertility as well as abdominal swelling (which they believed were "demonic fetuses"). However, by the twelfth century, C.E., the Jin dynasty physician Zhang Congzheng (ca. 1156-1228) recorded having a much more modern conception of the dream-waking consciousness relationship:

> He [Zhang Congzheng] recorded that for fifteen years a woman aged 34 dreamt about "sex with ghosts and deities" as well as scenes at a temple and in the underworld. Owing to her extreme emotions of fright and fear, she could not now get

pregnant. Other healers had applied ritual therapies including prayer and exorcisms to treat her, but none of them worked. Zhang diagnosed her malady as being cause by "repletion of phlegm in the chest" and treated her with a phlegm-expelling remedy. Afterwards, she had no dreams for ten days and, surprisingly, "conceived with one month." Along with the phlegm stagnation, Doctor Zhang concluded that the woman's long-term infertility did not originate in a "dream of sex with demons" itself, but in the emotional disturbances it caused.[300]

Thus, finally recognizing what the ancients foretold, physicians today now admit to the importance of prodromal dreams as "sleeping sonograms" of sorts, in the sense that pregnant women's dreams can unconsciously monitor their internally occurring biological changes—before diagnosis by any currently existing medical testing.

Native American

As is true of most Native American tribes, the Cherokees believed that shamanic visitations from deceased ancestors could provide medical assistance; however, they could also be the causes of illness and disease: "Death and illness were frequently attributed to recently deceased ghost relatives. When a child died, its ghost might appear to the mother in her dreams and try to draw her away to the 'darkening land' of the west; if she heeded these dreams, she would sicken and die."[301]
However, ancestors were not the only dream harbingers of ill health. "Dreams of snakes and other 'cold-blooded' animals and of human ghosts might also 'spoil the saliva' of the individual, who then become apathetic or despondent and slowly withers away.... To 'dream of different things' was another cause of illness; this often referred to the dreams of menstruating women, which were regarded as filled with unusual and vivid events, such as giving birth to a bear or to a litter of puppies...."[302]

Therefore, because of the complexity and enigmatic nature of dream messages, Native Americans relied upon the medical expertise of shamanic healers, who drew upon both material and the mythic culture to treat illness. Consequently, through what appears to be a precursory process of Freudian psychoanalysis, shamans would undertake extended periods of consultations with afflicted dreamers.

> ...[T]he dream or vision was the communicative medium that transferred the negative or positive power of the "cause" to the individual, not as a cause in itself, but as a consequence of being intimately bound to the mythic world. In this sense, dreams were *metonymic*, that is, they were sign-based and indexical of the entire schema of Cherokee religion and mythology. The dream as metonym was interpreted by the shaman, who sought out the "seat of pain" by questioning the ill person about their dreams over a period of months or even years in an attempt to find the "important thing." The dream was regarded as a far more significant indicator of the cause of an illness than any observable symptom....[303]

Native American healers stressed the importance of dream interpretation because they believed that through dreams, the mythic world communicated with waking consciousness, a complementary interaction which if misunderstood could, however, result in a "life and death" struggle:

> Dreams were "heralding events" that indicated the emotional engagement of the dreamer with the mythic world of religious belief.... In the full context of Cherokee healing, they were signs that the sacred powers were engaged in a struggle over the continued life of the individual. The dream typology of the shamans ranged from positive signs of healing, to sickness or possible death if the cause was not counteracted through the solicitation of a more powerful agency.... Thus dreams were the experiential basis of Cherokee healing.[304]

Through engagement with the mythical powers of Native American culture, dreamers themselves assisted shamans who utilized occult enchantments in conjunction with the effective application of herbal remedies. As in early Greco-Roman practices, plants were medicinal material, but among the Cherokee they were specifically identified according to their mythological association with the cause of a dreamer's disorder.

The plants fully participated in the sign-rich world of Cherokee healing. Once the cause of an illness was identified through dream analysis, it was related to certain types of plants named according to the qualities and appearances they contained in relationship to the mythic origin of the illness. Thus dreams indicating a negative agency of the powers of the deer or snake were remedied in part by the use of "Deer's Eye" or "Snake Tongue," plants so named because of their associations with those particular sacred powers....[305]

The shamanic connection to dream healing was not peculiar to the Cherokee; rather, this tribe is merely indicative of the widespread Native American belief in the dream as hermetic conduit to therapeutic remediation. In fact, widespread among Native American tribes, the call to become a shamanic healer was often received through a dream, especially via a visitation from an ancestor or through an incubated dream to invoke a spirit messenger.

In all regions, one of the main means of initiation as a shaman is through dreams. Among the Yurok and Wintu of California and the Paviostso of the Great Basin, a dead shaman may appear in a dream to a descendant, who will then assume the deceased's power. Such visions may come to a person while they are still a child. One Paviotso boy who wanted to become a shaman in order to cure the sick members of his community withdrew to a cave and prayed for the power to heal. Finally overcome by sleep, he had a vision of a healing session, in which a shaman was vainly attempting to revive a patient. The man died and the sleeper heard the lamentations of his family. Then the rock wall of the cave started to crack open, revealing the figure of a man holding the tail feather of an eagle (a common item in a shaman's sacred bundle). This spirit apparition then taught the boy the art of healing.[306]

This was also true among Mayan as well as Mesoamerican and Mexican indigenous cultures; shamanic healers of these societies were also chosen for and instructed in the medicinal arts by dream visitors, mostly with connections to natural environs and the earth, metaphorical references to the prehistoric Goddess traditions[307] that are embedded in Native American culture.

Throughout the Mayan area, shamans, who practice as healers and dream interpreters, are selected for these roles by giants [reminiscent of the Greek children of Gaia, the earth], dwarfs [symbol of those fascinated by earthly delights, as in the Indian iconography of "Dancing Shiva], and other tellurian deities who meet them when they are out walking in the hills and forests, visiting caves, or else while they are dreaming. Among the Tzotzil Maya…shamans receive their calling from these deities, who summon them to their mountain homes. There they are told that they have been chosen to become healers and are given patients to cure. In a series of dreams the candidate receives elaborate instruction concerning prayers, diagnostic information, and ritual procedure.[308]

Because of the great stresses dream healers suffered, a shaman would sometimes need support from senior practitioners, in much the same way that today psychoanalysts, themselves, must undergo a continual process of analysis. It is required that a currently practicing psychoanalyst continually seek assistance from more seasoned mentors. Similarly, Mayan dream healers also sought out the assistance of seniors:

"A shaman begins his or her practice informally by treating family members and neighbors. If he falls ill, or if social pressure builds for him to assume the public duties required of the role, he seeks out a senior shaman and tells him his dreams."[309]

Also suggestive of early Freudian dream theory is the Mayan focus on the importance of differentiating between the literal blatant and metaphorical occult dream images and the resultant need for a trained professional perspective to initiate healing. "The surface content of…dreams may involve such seemingly secular events as being chased by a horse or bull, but it is the *interpretation* of the dream symbols that matters."[310] As a result, recognizing the complementary nature of the individual's surface understanding of the dream with its symbolic references is essential for diagnosis and treatment. A trained shaman, as "diviner," dialogs with the patient to connect the "here and now" of the dreamer with the therapeutic, mythopoeic wisdom sources beyond temporal and spatial boundaries.

> …[D]iviners provide a surplus or superabundance of understanding for their clients. During the act of divination, individual creativity operates; jumbled ideas, metaphors and symbols suggest various possible interpretations which slowly give way to an ordered sequencing and to more limited interpretations. Finally, through dialogue between the diviner and the client, these interpretations are superseded by an unambiguous classification of the causes of the situation and the material needed to respond to and change it.[311]

Properly understood, the healing messages of mythopoeic dreams revealed medicinal cures that would not have otherwise been easily accessible to conscious waking life, as for example in this dream of a Blackfoot woman:

> Among the indigenous peoples of the Americas, divination often combines visualization and embodiment with the narration of myths. Knowledge of medicinal plants, for example, is often

received in dreams from animals. In one legend, a Blackfoot woman with tuberculosis noticed beaver tracks and left food for the animal, which returned the favour by appearing in her dreams to give her a cure for her illness. She tried the remedy—an infusion of lodge pole pin resin—while singing. After much vomiting, her chest cleared and she became well....This type of herbal knowledge received during dreams was not accepted unthinkingly but was subjected to empirical tests of its effectiveness.[312]

Such Native American recognition of the dream-waking continuum transforms time and space, creating a "continuous present," in which all is "one" in an atemporal and aspatial existence called the "Dream Time." Though suggestive of a biblical Eden, in that it was perfect, sans sickness and death, the Dream Time differs in that humans and animals are equal; no hierarchy exists. People are at one with all else. And no angel with a flaming sword stands guard to bar reentry. Rather, dreams are the open passageways through which any enlightened individual can freely travel.

Sadly, to our detriment, we have now fallen from this healing state, for too many turn their backs to the dream portals. However, such a paradise can be regained by simply awakening to the miraculous potentialities of our dreams. Through dreams, we as individuals and as a species can be restored. There is hope. Today, the ever increasing interest in dreams is reaching an all-time peak. Perhaps, one day soon, all medical personnel will not only carry stethoscopes, but also the ability to recognize the important wisdom of patients' dreams.

Modern/Contemporary Dream Healing

"To sleep, perchance to dream" is proving to be one of Shakespeare's most inspired reveries. Virtually each new day brings us closer to understanding the immense, therapeutic significance of dreams to sleep, not only for refreshing the mind but also for the wellbeing and preservation of the body. For example, dreams are proving essential to the maintenance of a functioning immune system—necessary for preserving physical health and sustaining the very life of an individual.

> ...[S]leep [and hence dreaming] is about more than just muscle relaxation or energy conservation, and there is now accumulating evidence of its role both in maintaining the immune system—through mechanisms such as cytokine signaling—and in optimizing cognitive functions, especially memory, notably through communication between the cortex and hippocampus. In particular, sleep is directly involved in the consolidation of memory from short to long term in humans.[313]

In fact, researchers at Stanford University studied the effects of circadian rhythm disruptions caused by sleep deprivation on fruit flies and determined that there is a "yin and yang" relationship of sorts most likely applicable to humans, proving the interrelatedness of normal sleep rhythms and a healthy immune system.

> Moreover, the study is of relevance to humans, claims one of its authors, Mimi Shirasu-Hiza from the Department of Microbiology and Immunology.... "I absolutely think this work is applicable to humans [...] In fact, parts of the immune system, like leukocyte activity, are already known to have circadian rhythm—that is, oscillate over 24 hours," she said. "There are many possible molecular signals to control these activities but it's often difficult to nail down exact causality in complex vertebrate systems. But, because the signaling pathways for both circadian biology and innate immunity are so highly conserved between flies and vertebrates, information from the fly is quite likely to help us understand how things work in humans," she said.[314]

Important for this study is the need to stress the necessity of dreaming during sleep. Succinctly, the purpose of sleep appears to be dreaming—"to sleep, perchance to dream"—both during REM [rapid eye movement] and non-REM stages. REM sleep accounts for only about one-fifth of total sleep time; however, experiments on rats proved that depriving them of REM sleep eventually led to the same negative health impacts as depriving them of *all* sleep. "Rats deprived only of REM sleep eventually develop the characteristics of total sleep deprivation— cognitive impairment, and increased heart rate, decreased body temperature, the development of ulcers and ultimately death...."[315]

Similarly, new discoveries in the field of REM dreaming have also revealed the connection of REM sleep to good health, especially regarding the importance of maintaining strong cognitive abilities in order to survive in an increasingly complex and ever dangerous technological age. Without a well-functioning mind, an individual is subject to numerous health and safety perils, including the potential of serious injury from accidents; for example, one moment of grogginess caused by sleep deprivation can cause the death of not only a motorist but also numerous innocent others.

Additionally, contemporary studies like those of Sarah Mednick (U. C. at San Diego) are now demonstrating the important connection of REM sleep states to fostering the mental acuity needed for healthy living. Mednick tested undergraduates by having them solve "association" word puzzles. Students were presented with such challenges as, what is the connection among these words: political, hat, birthday. (The answer is "party" as in political party, party hat, and birthday party.) After the testing session, students were separated into three groups: One third was allowed to nap and enter a REM dream state; one third was awakened right before the REM state; and one third was given the chance to just relax, but not sleep. Upon retesting, the two groups who were denied access to REM sleep both performed at lower levels than their initial testing; however, the students who had the benefit of even just a short period of REM dreaming outperformed their original scores by 40%--

thereby proving the important role of REM dreams in the overall process of sleeping.[316]

As important as REM dream stages are, non-REM dreaming is proving to be equally important to effecting healthy brain acuity as well as fortifying the immune system.[317] "...[I]t is non-REM sleep that is crucial for the day-to-day regulation of immunity, cognitive functions and probably development. This idea is strengthened by studies of the link between nonREM sleep and memory consolidation in humans, which have shown that although human performance at both mechanical and cognitive tasks is enhanced by sleep in general, non-REM sleep is most crucial."[318]

Robert Stickgold (Harvard Medical School) is studying the nature of non-REM sleep, and his findings are changing the way professionals think. In the past, REM sleep was believed to be the only time when one dreams; however, current research like Stickgold's has proven that dreams also occur during non-REM periods. And the two states have very different functions. Non-REM dreams are concerned with processing the daily seemingly impenetrable issues of our lives: the questions, challenges, stresses, and new experiences. The waking brain collects data that the non-REM dream stage then processes. In a sense, it asks what do I know, and how do I make sense of it, so I can use it in a constructive manner? To explain, Stickgold uses the example of a downhill skier, who during the day is confronted by a variety of hazardous obstacles. During non-REM sleep, the skier goes over his or her experiences and formulates ways of better negotiating these perplexing, dangerous hurdles. As Stickgold asserts, "Dreams help us perform better the next time."[319] Actually, if I may add, without dreams, there may not be a next time.

Recent research also points to the negative health effects of not being able to experience normal non-REM dreaming. A large number of severely depressed patients do not enter non-REM slow wave dream states; rather, they go straight to the REM stage and spend an unhealthy and inordinate time in this type of dreaming, thereby pointing to a physiological connection between clinical depression and an insufficient amount of non-REM dreaming, which is causing a chemical imbalance in the brain.[320] Similarly, non-REM disorders may also trigger chronic sleepwalking abnormalities. Guilleminault, et al. suggest a connection of the appearance of both "hypersynchronous slow delta" and "bursts of delta waves," Cyclical Alternating Patterns (CAP), during non-REM dream states with sleepwalking, pointing once again to the importance of dreams to maintaining and regulating the body's physical health systems.[321]

Ultimately, non-REM and REM dream states are proving to be essential to not only maintaining the health of an individual, but also to the preservation of the human species, itself. During non-REM states, dreamers process daily waking experiences and formulate potential strategies to deal with the most perplexing and potentially injurious threats. In "brainstorming" non-REM states, "anything goes," in that no strategy is disregarded, no matter how ludicrous it may prove to be. During REM states, dreamers safely "practice" activating these strategies in the safe environs of sleep, for no matter how ineffective a defense mechanism may be, the worst that could happen is that the dreamer awakens. Without the rehearsal function of dreams fostering memory and recall, *homo sapiens* would probably be extinct.

In addition to preserving healthy living, dreams may actually have the power to extend it. Researchers today are proving that there is a link between sleep and longevity. Public news bulletins currently abound regarding the health problems of either getting too much or too little sleep. Individuals who are sleep deprived (less than seven hours a night) suffer cognitive and physical maladies as well as secondary consequences, such as the possibility of accidents due to the deprivation. And individuals who sleep too much (over nine hours a night) have shortened life spans. But sadly these popular reports fail to stress the important role that dreams play during our sleeping states. It is not simply sleep—dreams are as fundamental to the sleep process as they are to the health of the body, a fact being realized today in the treatment of Post-Traumatic Stress Disorder (PTSD) and its resultant nightmares. PTSD nightmares are proving to be severely deleterious to the physical wellbeing of returning veterans and of women suffering the aftermath of physical and sexual abuses. Thus, it is of utmost importance to emphasize here that Post-Traumatic Stress Disorder is a somatic injury, as much damaging to the physical body as it is mentally agonizing.

Dreams and PTSD Trauma

> I have had a most rare vision. I have had a dream,
> past the wit of man to say what dream it was. Man
> is but an ass if he go about to expound this dream.
> Methought I was—there is no man can tell what.
> Methought I was—and methought I had—but man
> is but a patched fool if he will offer to say what
> methought I had. The eye of man hath not heard,
> the ear of man hath not seen, man's hand is not able
> to taste, his tongue to conceive, nor his heart to
> report, what my dream was (4.1.203-212).

Bottom in *A Midsummer Night's Dream*[322]

For the most part, returning veterans of the Vietnam War were not greeted with cheers and gratitude. When I returned, landing in Seattle, Washington for example, my small squad was unexpectedly met with vicious jeers and flung garbage. We thought we were heroes of a sort, but we were cursed, called "baby-killers" and other degrading epithets which I cannot include here. As a result, we huddled together, banishing and isolating ourselves, getting "wasted" in cheap, rented apartments. We didn't speak much. We cried even less. Mostly we just held it all in, words and tears alike. As we aged, we grew ill, both mentally and physically. Some committed suicide, perhaps to complete their self-seclusion.

Tom Holm, a Vietnam veteran of Cherokee-Creek heritage, narrates the Native American endurance exhibited by those returning braves from the horrors of war, but buried beneath the "strong hearts" of which he speaks is a hint of the self-seclusion, the dreadful realization of the irreparable pain each must carry alone:

> They came home individually, trickling back to their homes one by one. Some were immediately honored in their communities for taking part in the fighting in Vietnam. Some were ritually cleansed of the war's emotional effects. Some families ceremonially thanked those who had prayed for their loved one's safe return. Many—too many, perhaps—simply stored their uniforms in old trunks, attempted to take up life where they left off before their military service, and tried to forget the bloodletting and pain. It was a foregone conclusion that they would be unable to store the war away in a remote part of their minds. It had been too traumatic, too exciting, too terrifying and too intense an experience to ever block out or forget. There was certainly no dishonor in the way they fought, for they fought with tenacity, courage, and great skill. They had endured the filth, fatigue, fear, and fighting. Of the Native Americans it can truly be said: they indeed had strong hearts in Vietnam.[323]

Here, Holm openly acknowledges the "great irony" plaguing even those strong hearts: "But a great irony was in store for them. They had carried on an ancient tradition of arms and had performed well in combat, yet the U.S. military, by rotating them individually, not collectively, in and out of Vietnam, did that tradition a severe disservice. They returned separately, usually at night, slipping silently back home, just as their warrior ancestors had done only in defeat. While the war itself had been a shared experience—like a war party of old—the actual homecoming was not."[324]

Despite their loss of self, many decades later with much great hope, Vietnam veterans happily rejoiced at the turning tide of American sentiment toward our returning Middle East comrades because we thought and hoped that they would be spared from the lifelong self-seclusion we were forced to endure. With everyone else, we honored them and expressed our genuine, heartfelt gratitude for their service and sacrifices—proud of them and happy to have them safely back home. But sadly today, we are still suffering, for we are now feeling our and, tragically, their pain because so many—too many—of today's young veterans are suffering severe mental and physical problems, haunted by the horrific nightmares bred of Post-Traumatic Stress Disorder (PTSD) and the physical realities of self-seclusion and its resultant ultimate loss of self. So importantly and so tragically, this disabling "injury" afflicts not only male and female veterans, but also the many—too many— women and men who have been forced to suffer extreme sexual and physical abuse. This bodily trauma is why, please note, I have chosen to include PTSD in this first chapter on the medical healing potentialities of dreams because of its very somatic origin and its very real physiological consequences. Post-Traumatic Stress Disorder is an injury that cannot simply be defined as the product of mental stress—as so readily evidenced by the painful, physical effects engendered by the nightmares afflicting PTSD victims.

Nightmares and PTSD Nightmares

Nightmares are among the most prevalent symptoms reported by those who have suffered PTSD injuries. Tragically, however, PTSD nightmares differ markedly from so-called "normal" nightmare experiences. Ordinary nightmares are often therapeutic, in that they help reduce stress. To simplify, if the unconscious wishes to communicate a message "vital" to the survival of an individual, it could generate a nightmare to catch a dreamer's conscious attention. Nightmares are hard to ignore, let alone forget. Roberts, Lennings, and Heard explain Carl Gustav Jung's theory about the function of nightmares:

> Jung (1960) proposed that dreams perform a compensatory
> function in which repressed issues are exposed to the conscious

mind in imagery, aiding in the self-regulation of the unconscious by reducing the stress of keeping issues confined to the unconscious…. Nightmares, or anxiety dreams, are generated when the issue being presented has "vital significance" for the individual's life….[325]

Granted, while some current research challenges the hypothesis that nightmares are conducive to relieving stress, specifically citing the damaging anxiety generated by experiencing the nightmare itself, the prevailing traditional idea is supported by numerous studies; for example, Picchioni et al. conclude: "…[N]ightmares may provide a mechanism that supports our attempts to cope with stressful situations. In other words, perhaps the "coping" that occurs while we are asleep is reflective of a continuous process that works in conjunction with the coping we do when we are awake."[326]

In fact, the curative aspect of nightmares may actually be a product of hominid evolution, designed to support and maintain the propagation of our very species, itself. Antii Revonsuo is a professor of neuroscience at the University of Skovde (Sweden) and of psychology at the University of Turku (Finland). Revonsuo's research on nightmares supports traditional psychoanalytical, especially Jungian, theories that posit the unconscious to be a "vast and varied" store of wisdom into which we venture in our dream states. Revonsuo asserts that our nightmares, especially those of children, are the very same nightmares that our most ancient ancestors experienced; children's nightmares confront the same fears as those of primitive humans, for example franticly running from "big bad" wolves and desperately battling overpowering and frightening creatures—all very real occurrences in everyday prehistoric life.[327] Interestingly, decades ago, Desmond Morris identified serpents as the animal children most feared and concluded that this terror is inborn and culturally conditioned.[328] Thus, the dread of "snakes under the bed" and as horror figures in children's nightmares might be products of residual conditioning that created a collective unconscious formed when tree dwelling hominids feared sleep because of the one creature that could stealthily, silently breach their safe, lofty perches.

Revonsuo concludes that these nightmares manifest when we are very young because they are actually "rehearsals" for survival. By simulating threatening events, they teach us how to encounter them successfully in waking life. Therefore, nightmares are life-saving tools, for in these troubling dreams, we can practice survival techniques without the fear of destruction, for at worse, if a scheme does not work, we would simply awaken without injury. Furthermore, as Revonsuo observes, the nature of our nightmares changes as we grow older. As we age, the primitive objects of childhood fear are replaced by contemporary adult worries and situations, but the overall tactics of survival remain the same; only the personality of the "monsters in our closets" change.[329]

Contemporary neurological research supports the therapeutic potentialities of experiencing nightmares, even the extreme waking-nightmares of those suffering from Sleep Paralysis, as products of evolutionary body-brain processes. According to Cheyne: "That primitive cognitive concerns are associated with REM-related hallucinations should not be surprising, given evolutionary perspectives on REM and dreaming. Clearly, the essence of w-nightmare [waking-nightmares] as we have found it consists of the most intense experiences of agent-related danger as well as of radical vestibular-motor experiences".[330]

Beginning with the most primitive of humanoid species, the body's physical interaction with the perplexing perils of the waking world has continuously fashioned and refashioned the complexities of the brain's neural structures. As a result, the concept of "self" is not simply a mental or spiritual construct. Rather, through its suffering of the "slings and arrows of outrageous fortune," the body has shaped the neurological systems of our brains as well as the narrative content of our dreams and nightmares. Dreams, especially our highly animated nightmares, are creative enterprises rooted in the brain; specifically,

Edward Pace-Schott identifies the mPFC (Medial Prefrontal Cortex), associated with slow-wave delta NREM (non-REM) sleep, as the "encephalonic" locus of our creativity and an area that is often implicated in the process of narrative construction.[331] Thus, from this perspective, dreams can be viewed as physical as well as mental and spiritual compositions formulated in protective response to the actions of environmental causations.

Although not all environmental dangers are agent-related, threatening agents have, in the course of evolution, constituted an important and special category of both interspecific and intraspecific threat. Another central concern of consciousness is that of the bodily self and changes in its relation to the external world. The neural substrate of this concern is an interconnected matrix of motor, proprioceptive, and vestibular structures. In at least one sense the self does have a center. It is the body and that body has a neural representation.[332]

Dreams are as much a product of the body as are the somatic phenomena of waking life. As Pace-Schott concludes, the "one brain is responsible for both waking and dream states."[333]

Tragically, however, any therapeutic value of nightmares is completely lost by and negated in the nightmares of those suffering PTSD. For the most part, "In contrast, recurring nightmares in PTSD patients appear to reinforce the memory of the trauma and contribute to the dreamer's distress."[334] Rather than functioning as evolutionary media to minimize stress, PTSD nightmares are predominantly physical recreations of the original traumatic bodily experiences. Admittedly, however, PTSD nightmares are not solely limited to representations of the original traumas. As Mellman and Pigeon assert, comprehensive evaluations of chronic PTSD patients reveal that traumatic memories are not the exclusive type of dreaming.[335] Nevertheless, Mellman and Pigeon do conclude that for all PTSD victims, whatever the cause—be it, for example, rape, acts of war, escapes from fires and natural disasters, or kidnapping—an overwhelming amount of nightmares demonstrate an origin in the precipitating traumatic event:

> …[E]xposed populations tend to report dreams with specific trauma-related or thematically related content during the acute aftermath of disasters and other traumas, and dreams that are similar to the memory of the actual traumatic event are associated with the development of PTSD. Chronic PTSD is associated with recurring dreams that represent specific memories of a traumatic experience.[336]

More specifically, in contrast to the nightmares of nonPTSD sufferers, a majority (approximately 71-96%) of returning war veterans relate nightmares that involve replication or near replication of their war experiences.[337] In fact, medical professionals are often alerted to PTSD by the severity of a patient's nightmares. As a result, clinicians often recognize PTSD in patients because of the severity of flashbacks and disturbing images, which result in emotional and behavioral disorders and a heightening of arousal.[338]

PTSD nightmares also differ from normal "bad dreams" in that they often occur earlier in the night, during different stages of sleep and are more likely to be accompanied by body movements. As a result, PTSD can create high levels of sleep-disordered breathing problems, most notably sleep apnea, resulting in actual physiological reactions to perceived fears, including profuse sweating and racing heartbeats. Additionally, traumatic re-experiencing of painful incidents can be triggered by waking sensory stimuli, such as sights, smells or sounds. As a result, PTSD disrupts the lives of sufferers in that it causes them to withdraw from everyday experiences in an effort to avoid events, areas, and even emotions that can too painfully "bring it all back." Consequently, PTSD sufferers can feel overwhelmed and anxious, irritable and easily prone to aggressive physical behavior as well as emotional outbursts.[339] I have been able to observe this hyper-arousal state in the near paranoia of my student-veterans, who remain subconsciously "on guard" from what they perceive to be the uncomfortable environment of the classroom, where they nervously fidget and protectively sit backs against the wall with the doorway kept in full sight.

Fortunately, despite the severity of these nightmares and their negative physical distress, there is hope! Because PSTD is an injury, the possibility for healing is not just a dream. Contemporary clinicians are now experimenting with pharmaceuticals—so reminiscent of the ancients' use of herbal pharmacology, often in conjunction with Imagery Rehearsal Therapy (IRT).

Pharmaceuticals, IRT, and Lucid Dreaming

Though little research is currently available regarding the effectiveness of medications to treat PTSD, according to the National Center for PTSD, prazosin is showing some promise. Prazosin, an antihypertensive, belonging to the alpha-blocker family of drugs, is commonly used for treating high blood pressure.[340] It is now proving effective for PTSD sufferers because their bodies release too much adrenaline, which the prazosin blocks by reducing the amount of norepinephrine believed to be causally associated with nightmares and other sleep disturbances. However, prazosin is not without side-effects and drug interactions. For instance, antidepressants are also utilized to treat PTSD, but prazosin cannot be used in conjunction with trazodone, an antidepressant prescribed to stimulate the mood of PTSD patients and to restore the levels of serotonin in the brain. Therefore, medical practitioners need to explore the use of other antidepressants which have been approved by the Food and Drug Administration (FDA), for example sertraline (Zoloft) and paroxetine (Paxil).

Conversely, other pharmaceuticals are not proving to be effective treatment alternatives; for example, according to Mellman and Pigeon, both guanfacine and cyproheptadine have not proven to work.

And claims of the effectiveness of "novel antipsychotic medications, antidepressants that feature postsynaptic serotonin antagonism (trazondone and nefazodone)…" have not been substantiated.[341]

As a result, drug therapies need to be complemented by nightmare reduction methodologies, such as Imagery Rehearsal Therapy (IRT). Simply put, IRT requires sufferers to "rewrite" the scripts of their nightmares and reinforce the new dream scenarios by continually replaying their rescripted nonthreatening ending. Germain, et al., explain: "Briefly, IRT involves the imaginal rehearsal of a new dream (ND) that is non-distressing and that the patient elaborates by altering elements of the original NM [nightmare] scenario. IRT does not involve imaginal exposure to the NM or traumas and does not directly promote abreaction."[342]

To prove the effectiveness of Imagery Rehearsal Therapy, Germain, et al. utilized IRT as treatment for 44 women suffering from PTSD caused by sexual assault. Their nightmares were creating conditions of poor physical health as well as increasing the severity of psychiatric distress. Therapy involved small group sessions conducted over two three-hour periods, and participants were instructed to keep dream logs. The results were positive, in that patients—regardless of the kind of trauma endured and relived—did diminish the amount and severity of their nightmares, pointing to the efficacy of combining IRT in conjunction with pharmaceutical treatment procedures: " …[S]ome patients with PTSD may significantly benefit from adjunctive NM-focused interventions to complement other pharmacological or cognitive-behavioral treatment strategies aimed at reducing daytime PTSD symptoms."[343]

Similarly, lucid dreaming is an effective technique that allows nightmare sufferers to consciously enter their dreams to rescript their content—in essence enabling the waking body to spontaneously enter the unconscious realm, thereby creating an especially unique psychophysiological state.

Lucid dreaming refers to a specific dream state characterized by the dreamer's awareness of being in a dream and the ability to volitionally control its contents. Lucid dreamers report being in possession of all their cognitive faculties: they are able to reason clearly, to remember the conditions of waking life, and to act voluntarily within the dream upon reflection or in accordance with plans decided upon before sleep…. The dream state can be experienced very vividly, and thus lucid dreams are often described as peak experiences or "high" dreams….[344]

Holzinger, LaBerge, and Levitan utilized polysomnographic recordings to explore the electrophysiological differences between lucid and nonlucid REM dream states. They discovered that EEG (Electroencephalogram) signals revealed an increase in the beta-a frequency band during lucid dreaming most notably in the "left parietal lobe (P3), an area of the brain considered to be related to sematic [a warning or signal of danger] understanding and awareness."[345] Thus, through lucid dreaming, nightmare suffering can be reduced on the mental and physical levels, for trauma has two dimensions: 1) the distress experienced during the nightmare, and 2) the subsequent physiological disorders experienced during waking life. As a result, alleviating nightmare traumas helps relieve waking physical and psychological maladies in normal dreamers and PTSD sufferers.

Dreams and Bodily Health

As Shakespeare so eloquently proclaims, sleep and "what dreams may come" (3.1.67)[346] during it are indeed the "…the chief nourisher in life's feast (2.2.44)"[347] In fact, contemporary research is proving that the normal patterns of the sleep cycle, including non-REM and REM dreaming, are essential for the maintenance and continuance of life itself, even down to the very chromosomal composition of our genes. "Descriptive data continue to accrue to suggest that sleep disturbance in late life might carry its own morbidity and should not be dismissed by the sleep medicine specialist. New data suggest that the breakdown of sleep in the aged organism might reflect physiologic age and reflect alterations in function present at the genomic level."[348]

As a result, sleep deprivation and dream disruptions are associated with such chronic health conditions as diabetes, cardiovascular irregularities, and hypertension. And sleep/dream disorders are one of the major causes of accidents at home, on the road, and in the workplace, especially among night shift workers and those whose employment schedules are always changing, many of whom, ironically, are in positions of safeguarding public safety and wellbeing, for example airline personnel, police, EMT first responders, firefighters, nurses, and doctors.[349] Walsh, Dement, and Dinges further propose that adolescents and young adults, notably including college students, are particularly subject to sleep-dream deprivations which precariously expose them, as a result, to the dangers of suffering serious, possibly fatal, injuries due to accidents as well as to severe health threats like addiction to depressants and stimulants.[350]

Additionally, Michael Lowis reaffirms the body-mind connection proposed by Jung (and to some degree Freud), when he asserts that, "…[D]reams do have the potential to inform mental and physical well-being."[351] So the sooner one listens to the health-related messages of one's dreams, the better chance one has of healing: "Indeed, correctly identified, the information conveyed in dreams can provide early warnings of threats to both physical and mental well-being that might not become obvious during waking life until much later, when the problem could be significantly more debilitating and difficult to remedy."[352]

Such informative dreams are categorized as "prodromal," in that they can bring to consciousness irregularities in the body's biochemical and physiological structures. During pregnancy, for example, many women experience powerfully vivid dreams, which are often associated with fetus development as well as being reflections of the hormonal and physiological changes they are, themselves, experiencing. Coo, Milgrom, and Trinder tested this supposition that the dreams of antenatal and postnatal women were expressions of changes experienced during their transitions to motherhood[353] and concluded that:

>...[T]he findings of this study support the continuity hypothesis of dreaming by suggesting that dreams of pregnant women reflect some of the changes inherent to the transition to motherhood; the analysis of postnatal dreams indicates that these changes remain stable up to three months after childbirth. The pattern of dream content is consistent with the motherhood constellation model in its description of some of the aspects that are necessary for a successful transition to motherhood, such as awareness of the unborn and newborn baby, an enhancement of protective functions to take care of an infant, and a strong focus on family members.[354]

Although dreaming intensity may be heightened during pregnancy, prodromal dreams are not only experienced by expectant mothers. For example, I once dreamt of a ragged-edged sphere, pock-mocked like a planetoid bombarded with meteorites, bathed in bright light. I had no idea what this dream meant, but it was perplexing and lingered with me for a long time. Then, during a routine check-up, an ultrasound screening revealed the presence of a gall stone. After the surgery, the doctor showed me an x-ray of its image, which to my amazement, exactly replicated the one in my dream. Similarly, dreams can also reflect the impaired health conditions of anorexics and bulimics as well as predict the levels of their desire to be healed. Roger Knudson's case study of the dream of Stephanie, an anorexic, makes a strong case for the importance of understanding the anorexic's physical "experience" of her dream, rather than focusing on an interpretive metaphorical analysis of it: " Understood in terms of presentational rather than representational symbolism, the dream provided a bridge between

Stephanie's conscious mind, purged of all passions, and her starving, increasingly numb body. In that bridging, the dream reanimated both!"[355]

Such an understanding of dreams as "bridges," in this case from Stephanie's anorexic body to her conscious mind, enabled Knudson to conclude that:

The life of the dream is not something produced by our interpretive efforts. Rather it is the dream that arrives fully animated and, if only the interpretative impulse can be postponed, that has the potential to animate the dreamer's experience. For Stephanie, it was the dream as dreamed, *prior to* any interpretation, that was revivifying, rejuvenating. In Stephanie's view, the dream was enlivening and in the context of her anorexia may well have been life saving.

The mythologist Joseph Campbell (1988) once said, "People say that what we're all seeking is a meaning for life. I think that what we're seeking is an experience of being alive, so that our life experiences on the purely physical plane will have resonance within our innermost being and reality, so that we actually feel the rapture of being alive."

In concert with Campbell, what Stephanie needed was not an interpretation of her dream, a meaning. It was the experience of being alive![356]

Furthering the identity of dreams as physiological bridges connecting somatic functions to consciousness, Leland van den Daele defines dreaming as a rational process of the brain's right hemisphere, designed to preserve and maintain the health of the body by enhancing its ability to awaken to survival adaptations related by the nondominant hemisphere.

Although the role and importance of the interpretation of dreams has been deemphasized in clinical discussions for the past several decades, new models of dream physiology suggest the central role and importance of dreams in the regulation of behavior.... A review of the neurophysiological literature pertinent to direct interpretation suggests dreams are sustained by midbrain anatomical networks with feed-back and feed-forward links to the cortex. The anatomical networks are termed the endogenous-intraorganismic system, the exogenous-transactional system, and the relational system that correspond to subjective, objective, and relational dreams in direct interpretation. Just as ordinary thought is the province of the dominant or left hemisphere, dreams are the province of the nondominant or right hemisphere.[357]

Yet the role of dreaming is much more important than simply functioning as a bridge to unconscious somatic processes. Dreams are actually essential to preserving life. Sleep and the dream cycle that structures it are proving to be a vital process, essential for good brain health and ultimately the survival of the body itself. Lulu Xie, et al. posit that: "...[S]leep has a critical function in ensuring metabolic homeostasis.... Thus, the restorative function of sleep may be a consequence of the enhanced removal of potentially neurotoxic waste products that accumulate in the awake central nervous system."[358]

In their effort to understand the answer to one of the "greatest mysteries in biology"—Why is sleep restorative?—Xie et al. had to first acknowledge the life-threatening physiological dangers of sleep deprivation: "Sleep deprivation reduces learning, impairs performance in cognitive tests, prolongs reaction time, and is a common cause of seizures.... In the most extreme case, continuous sleep deprivation kills rodents and flies within a period of days to weeks.... In humans, fatal familial or sporadic insomnia is a progressively worsening state of sleeplessness that leads to dementia and death within months or years...."[359]

Second, they then discovered that, unlike peripheral tissue surrounding the brain, which has lymph vessels to evacuate "excess interstitial proteins" for "degradation in the liver," the brain, "….[D]espite its high metabolic rate and the fragility of neurons to toxic waste products, the brain lacks a conventional lymphatic system."[360] Consequently, their research led them to identify the vital importance of sleep as the essential "cleansing agent" for removing waste products from the brain. As a result, Xie et al. interestingly reiterate the intuitive wisdom of Shakespeare's words, when they also come to the conclusion that sleep is indeed a "balm of hurt minds":

> Because of the high sensitivity of neural cells to their environment, it is essential that waste products of neural metabolism are quickly and efficiently removed from the brain interstitial space….The existence of a homeostatic drive for sleep—including accumulation of a "need to sleep" substance during wakefulness that dissipates during sleep—has been proposed…. Because biological activity is inevitably linked to the production of metabolic degradations products, it is possible that sleep subserves the important function of clearing multiple potentially toxic CNS waste products…. The purpose of sleep has been the subject of numerous theories since the time of the ancient Greek philosophers….An extension of the findings reported here is that the restorative function of sleep may be due to the switching of the brain into a functional state that facilitates the clearance of degradation products of neural activity that accumulate during wakefulness.[361]

As more and more contemporary scientific research is revealing, dreams can, indeed, help physicians to diagnose and understand physiological diseases and conditions. Walsh, Dement, and Dinges, for instance, identify sleep deprivation (and thereby dream disruption) to be one of the major causes of obesity and diabetes. "An epidemiologic study found sleep durations less than 6 or more than 9 hours to be associated with an increased prevalence of diabetes and impaired glucose tolerance. A growing body of evidence also supports a link between sleep-disorder breathing and insulin resistance, independent of degree of obesity. Thus, both short sleep and disrupted sleep associated with sleep-disordered breathing appear to be associated with endocrine and metabolic changes that may promote obesity and diabetes."[362] In turn, obesity and diabetes are linked to hypertension and cardiovascular disease—so are sleep disorders and dreams.

Citing the extremely high mortality rates of cardiovascular disease and hypertension (responsible for 35%-56% of all mortalities) among Americans, Shahrokh Javaheri stresses the importance of understanding the strong connection of these killers to sleep disorders, specifically to sleep apnea:

Obstructive sleep apnea is associated with a number of biochemical and cellular abnormalities. Obstructive apnea results in neurohormonal activation; release of inflammatory mediators such as cytokines; increased expression of adhesion molecules, resulting in attachment of white blood cells to endothelial cells and their transmigration; and oxidative stress.... Through increased production of reactive oxygen species, a number of transcription factors are activated, increasing the expression of redox-sensitive genes and resulting in the production of vasoactive and inflammatory proteins. These reactions underlie the pathologic process involved in endothelial dysfunction syndrome, the underlying pathophysiological mechanism for atherosclerosis, hypertension, stroke, heart failure, and coronary artery disease...[363]

Sleep apnea is intimately associated with the disruption of dream cycles. This disruption, as perilous as it may be for the heart, in turn, also prevents the brain (as discussed above) from cleansing destructive waste products and abnormalities. Consequently, it is important here to stress the point that sleep alone is not restorative. Sleep exists to allow for nonREM and REM dreaming. Subjects permitted to sleep for long periods of time, but who were awakened whenever they entered dream states, experienced the same range of health threats that sleep deprived patients endure—for example, endocrine disorders that are in turn linked to hypothyroidism, diabetes, obesity, and sex hormone maladies.[364]

Importantly, Verrier and Mittleman draw the vital connection between sleep disorders and dreaming, especially in regard to heart health. The normal nonREM and REM dream stages essential for healthy brain functioning ironically place stresses on the heart, which for those suffering with cardiac disease are life threatening.

The brain, in subserving its need for periodic re-excitation during rapid eye movement (REM) sleep and dreaming, imposes significant demands on the heart by inducing bursts of sympathetic nerve activity, which reaches levels higher than during wakefulness. In patients with cardiac disease, such neural activity may compromise coronary artery blood flow, as metabolic demand outstrips supply, and may trigger sympathetically mediated life-threatening arrhythmias in response to functional myocardial ischemia. An additional challenge is presented by non-REM sleep, when hypertension may lead to malperfusion of the heart and brain as a result of a lowered blood pressure gradient through stenosed vessels. Impairment of ventilation by sleep-related breathing disorders, including obstructive sleep apneas and central sleep apneas, which afflict millions of Americans, can generate reductions in arterial oxygen saturation and other pathophysiological sequelae.[365]

So treating cardiovascular disease by regulating continuous positive airway pressure (CPAP) helps restore heart health which, in turn, also helps restore the dream cycles that are imperative for brain health. Sleep and dreams are complements of one process, so health depends on the normal functioning of both.

Sleep disorders and dream disruption appear to be causative factors of fatigue in cancer patients, who often experience disturbances in the normal circadian rhythm of sleep/wake cycles. Thus, overwhelming feelings of tiredness throughout the day and night can cause patients to experience incomplete sleep patterns, thereby preventing them from benefiting from the therapeutic nature of sleep and dreams. Disrupted sleep and dream cycles degrade patients' quality of life as well as their response to, and toleration of, treatment.[366] Similarly, fibromyalgia and chronic fatigue syndrome may also be associated with sleep and dream disturbances. In fact, MacFarlane and Moldofsky identify "unrefreshing sleep" as a "key component" of these syndromes. They suggest the use of sleep electroencephalograms (EEG) to detect nonperiodical arousals in order to determine if a relationship between them and episodic sleep disruptions can be identified.[367] Succinctly, irregular awakenings interfere with the normal sleep/dream cycles which, in turn, result in fatigue.

What the Future May Bring

Technology, especially regarding electronic media, is a major factor in the lives of most contemporary Americans; however, nothing in our past has really prepared us for both the potentially life-altering changes ahead and, more importantly, for the rapidity of these changes. Over forty years ago, Alvin Toffler wrote about the "future shock" inevitably resultant due to the inability of the finite human psychology and physiology to keep pace with ever increasing technological changes, especially since a great deal of their upheaval is not mandated by human need. Sadly, as any teacher or parent can attest, today's youths are almost "lost" in virtual reality—most seriously in video gaming as well as in altered forms of communication and human relationships.

To verify the results of recent but rare studies concerning the effects of electronic media on the sleeping/dreaming patterns of adolescents and teens, Jan Van den Bulck researched the impact of media viewing on the dreams of thirteen and sixteen year old students. She found that the amount of media usage is less of a factor than the overall effect of any level of indulgence in TV and video gaming. As she asserts, "Media influence on dream content was not limited to excessive media users."[368] She concludes that, regardless of intensity of usage, television and computer games can produce nightmares as well as "pleasant" dreams, illustrating the influence of media on both. Thus, television viewing and video gaming disrupt the normal sleep patterns of children and teens, who overindulge in the use of such media causing bouts of sleep deprivation:

> TV viewing and computer game play have been linked to sleeping problems. It has been well documented that both computer games and TV contain a lot of potentially frightening messages. The present study tried to ascertain the prevalence of nightmares related to TV viewing and game play. TV content shows up frequently in nightmares…in older boys. Computer game play does not have the same frequency as TV viewing; levels are much lower. Nevertheless, about 1 in 10 boys reports having game-related nightmares. …[T]he numbers certainly should give pause to people concerned about the mental well-being of children.[369]

Ironically, this embracing of the "dark side" of technologically is nowhere better illustrated than by media itself—for instance, by Darth Vader from the *Star Wars* series. The original film, guided by the works of comparative mythologist Joseph Campbell, portrays Vader as the man given over to the "force"; that is, he is the human who loses his humanity to the machine. His body is molded plastic, and his voice is mechanically amplified. On the surface, he appears invincible, but when his mask is removed, there appears a withered, blanched barely human creature, and where the mask chaffs his face, his skin is irritated and scarred. Like Mary Shelley's Dr. Frankenstein's monster, he is a metaphor to illustrate the self-destructive nature of "science" out of control.

However, as ominous as Toffler's prediction of "future shock" may prove to be, there is a proverbial "silver lining." Dreams are infinite; thus, they are our most authentic hope of not only adapting to the rapidity of sometimes unwanted and senseless change, but also of harnessing all the positive elements of technological innovations. For example, media usage appears to improve lucid dreaming, a powerful therapeutic tool. By learning how to consciously enter one's dreams, one can rescript painful nightmares, restore restful sleep, and adapt dreams to solve problems. Jayne Gackenbach examined the morning-after dreams of avid video gamers and posits that such participation with electronic media results in increased abilities for lucid dreaming. Mindful of earlier research proving that video gaming keeps children awake, Gackenbach focused on "well-rested" gamers. She was able to identify a positive correlation between "gamers" and increased abilities for lucid dreaming. "In a factor analysis, lucid and control dreams were associated with all electronic media use but most strongly with video game play."[370]

In an earlier study, Gackenbach presented the hypothesis that the stimulation of lucid dreaming by video gaming—especially among very active gamers—had a positive effect on consciousness development. As she explains, qualitative cognitive improvements continue through the verbal to higher stages:

These nonverbal or nonlinear levels are thought to be characterized by spatial thinking, multimodal speeding of processing, and the integration of self and affect with cognition. Thus, this developmental sequence is described in terms of consciousness and not just cognition in order to capture the breadth of the phenomena. Theorists suggest that exposure to appropriate amplifiers is necessary to move to the next higher level of consciousness (Alexander et al., 1990). In the past these amplifiers have included meditation and prayer, recall of dreams and self-reflection among others. In this study, it is suggested that video game play may be another such amplifier.[371]

Nevertheless, Gackenbach admonishes that: "The bottom line is that children through young adults are highly involved in video game play, and it is thus incumbent upon us to be more sensitive to what video game play is doing to the development of consciousness."[372]

As a result, Gackenbach teamed with Arielle Boyes to expand her original video gamer control group to include users of additional electronic media devices, including social media, wireless access, and texting/tweeting. They determined that, "Although there were meaningful differences…most analysis resulted in no differences in dreams. Differences seemed to support the nightmare protection thesis of video game play…."[373] This study appears to support the nightmare protection function to reinforce the hypothesis that contemporary overdependence on, and excessive usage of, video gaming and other electronic media are altering the processes of consciousness development among future generations. One such danger may be a correlation between violent video gaming and aggressive behavior; however, more research is needed.

Consequently, technological advancements are changing the landscape of dreaming and altering the way researchers now approach the discipline. Nevertheless, the science of sleep/dream medicine is theoretically in its infancy. Fortunately, however, the contemporary interest in sleep medicine is ever increasing; as a result, more and more studies are shining proverbial "light" upon the deepest mysteries of our nocturnal journeys into the darkness of unconsciousness. One example of what the future holds is the hypothesis that we may potentially have the ability to reconstruct the visual images of our dreams and project them as movies. For the most part, the technology already exists but does need a lot of refinement and much more development. In neuroscientist Jack Gallant's laboratory, a University of California, Berkeley research team is using magnetic resonance imaging combined with computer modeling to reconstruct visual brain images. To date, they report that, although it is now only possible to reconstruct movie clips that subjects have already watched, the potential is there to project memories and dreams. In support of their assertion, this team of Berkeley researchers summarize the progress they have already made to overcome some existing technological shortcomings:

> Recent functional magnetic resonance imaging (fMRI) studies have modeled brain activity elicited by static visual patterns and have reconstructed these patterns from brain activity…. However, blood oxygen level-dependent (BOLD) signals measured via fMRI are very slow…, so it has been

difficult to model brain activity elicited by dynamic stimuli such as natural movies. Here we present a new motion-energy…encoding model that largely overcomes this limitation. The model describes fast visual information and slow hemodynamics by separate components. We recorded BOLD signals in occipitotemporal visual cortex of human subjects who watched natural movies and fit the model separately to individual voxels. Visualization of the fit models reveals how early visual areas represent the information in movies. To demonstrate the power of our approach, we also constructed a Bayesian decoder…by combining estimated encoding models with a sampled natural movie prior. The decoder provides remarkable reconstructions of the viewed movies. These results demonstrate that dynamic brain activity measured under naturalistic conditions can be decoded using current fMRI technology.[374]

Sadly, the images are still very sketchy and blurry so as of now, the potentiality of projecting our dreams appears to remain an achievement reserved for the distant future. Still, the therapeutic advantages of this process are well worth pursuing, for the ability to project dreams and memories will, for instance, assist medical practitioners to help patients with brain disorders. According to Jean Thilmany: "The technology could give doctors and scientists a better understanding of what goes on in the minds of stroke victims, coma patients, and others who can't speak. It may also lay the groundwork for a brain-machine interface so that people with cerebral palsy or paralysis, for example, can guide computers with their minds."[375]

Scientists are coming to realize that dreams continually prove to be one of the "royal roads" to achieving physical wellness in the future. Contemporary research is also coming to recognize, through science and technology, what the ancients intuited: the immense importance of understanding dreams. Through dreams, we awaken to the healing potentialities of the body-mind-spirit synthesis, as essential for the wellness of each individual as it is for the propagation of all humanity itself.

ABOUT THE AUTHOR

Dr. Francesco Ancona is a Professor of English, Sussex County College since 1991; courses taught include "The Interpretation of Dreams," "Myth, Dream, and Image," and introduction to comparative mythologies. He is the author of several books: *Writing the Absence of the Father: Undoing Oedipal Structures in the Contemporary American Novel* (UPA); *Myth: Matter of Mind?* (UPA); *Crisis in America: Father Absence* (Nova Sciences); *Femina Sapiens: Were Women the First Truly Thinking Human Beings?* (Wyndham Hall) and *He Says/She Says Shakespeare* (UPA).

His education includes Doctor of Medical Humanities, Drew University; Doctor of Arts, St. John's University; M.A. in English, Montclair State University; and a B.A. in American Studies, Ramapo State College. Dr. Ancona has also trained in psychoanalysis at Centenary College and the Academy of Clinical and Applied Psychoanalysis. He served as a McGraw Center Faculty Fellow at Princeton University and is a former Assistant Editor of the *Journal of Evolutionary Psychology*. He has been cited for teaching excellence by the NJ Council for County Colleges and is a member of the International Association for the Study of Dreams.

ENDNOTES

---

[1] Philip R. Lehrman was the first to quote this in "Freud's Contributions to Science" *Harofe Haivri*, vol. 1 (1940), but the citation in better recognized by its later citation in Lionel Trilling's "Freud and Literature," *The Liberal Imagination* (NY: RB Classics paperback, 1950), 34.

[2] A discussion of the "dream-work" will be presented later in this chapter.

[3] Thus, the association of prehistoric art with dreams will be discussed in Chapter Three: Dreams and Spiritual Health.

[4] J. Donald Hughes, "A History of Dream Interpretation in Western Civilization from the Earliest Times Through the Middle Ages" (unpublished paper, Univ. of Denver, December 1984).

[5] Hughes.

[6] Curtiss Hoffman, "Dumuzi's Dream: Dream Analysis in Ancient Mesopotamia," *Dreaming: Journal of the Association for the Study of Dreams* 14.4 (December 2004), 240-41.

[7] Hoffman, 241.

[8] Hughes.

[9] The professionally trained "analyst based" interpretation of dreams later found many detractors, including some of Freud's own disciples.

[10] The papyrus, circa 1300 B.C.E., is named after Chester Beatty, who donated it to the British Museum; however, it is believed to be a copy of a much older version, possibly dating to 2000 B. C. E.

[11] Nancy McWilliams, *Psychoanalytic Diagnosis: Understanding Personality Structure in the Clinical Process* (NY: The Guilford Press, 1994), 131.

[12] McWilliams, 132.

[13] McWilliams, 132.

[14] A pre-dream practice to allow for the control of dream content; for example, through incubation, a dreamer could focus on a specific topic to facilitate the solving of perplexing waking issues.

[15] Hughes.

¹⁶ Gregory Shushan, "Greek and Egyptian Dreams in Two Ptolemaic Archives: Individual and Cultural Layers of Meaning," *Dreaming: Journal of the Association for the Study of Dreams* 16.2 (June 2006), 140.

¹⁷ The important metaphorical nature of serpents as Goddess-tradition "healing" symbols is discussed in Chapter Four, as is the origin of their appearance on the rod of Asclepius, the god's emblem.

¹⁸ *Iamata* are a collection of about 70 narratives from pilgrims, who journeyed to Epidauros, testifying to the miraculous cures of Asklepious.

¹⁹ Louise Cilliers and Francois Pieter Retief, 86.

²⁰ Not to be confused with Artemidorus Ephesius, a second to first century B.C.E. geographer of the same name.

²¹ Christine Walde, 133.

²² Delaney, *All About Dreams,* CA: HarperSanFrancisco, 1998: 24.

²³ Delaney, *All About Dreams,* 18.

²⁴ Delaney, *All About Dreams,* 30.

²⁵ The roots of the Taoist tradition are believed to be prehistoric and part of Chinese folklore.

²⁶ Delaney, *All About Dreams,* 30.

²⁷ Freud actually completed *The Interpretation of Dreams* in 1899 but delayed publication until 1900 so as to demonstrate its ushering in of a new century, possibly not realizing that the new century actually began with 1901.

²⁸ Charles Brenner, *An Elementary Textbook of Psychoanalysis,* revised/expanded ed. (NY: Anchor Books: 1974), 12.

²⁹ Freud's wish fulfillment theory of dreams can actually be perceived as three-fold: satisfaction dreams, impatience dreams (where one anxiously awaits an anticipated event), and comfort dreams.

³⁰ The devastation of World War I and the death of his beloved daughter Sophie played heavily upon Freud's mind; more so, the dreams of returning veterans were perplexing in that these veterans re-experienced in their dreams the horrors they had witnessed and/or suffered through. How could these repletion nightmares possibly be wish fulfillments? In *Beyond the Pleasure Principle*, Freud explains that he observed little Ernst, his eighteen-month old grandson (Sophie's child), playing at what Freud

came to term the *"fort—da"* game. Whenever Ernst's mother was absent, Ernst would toss a wooden spool, around which he had tied a bit of string, out of his crib. Every time he tossed it away, he would cry *"fort"* (meaning gone); then he would pull it back and chuckle *"da"* (there). Through the repletion of loss and return, he compensated for his mother's absence, assuring himself that like the spool, she too would return.

[31] William Shakespeare, *The Complete Works of Shakespeare*, 5th ed. Bevington, David, ed. (NY: Pearson-Langham, 2003), 1119.

[32] Shakespeare, 1102.

[33] Brenner, 11.

[34] Freud, *The Interpretation of Dreams*, in *The Basic Writings of Sigmund Freud*, ed. and trans. A. A. Brill (NY: The Modern Library, 1938), renewed 1966, 319.

[35] Freud, "An Autobiographical Study," in *The Freud Reader*, ed. Peter Gay (NY: Norton, 1995), 28-29.

[36] Carl G. Jung, *Man and his Symbols* (NY: Anchor Press, Doubleday, 1964), p. 27.

[37] Freud, *The Interpretation of Dreams*, 322.

[38] Freud, *The Interpretation of Dreams*, 322-36.

[39] Freud, *The Interpretation of Dreams*, 316.

[40] Nancy McWilliams, 130.

[41] See specifically *Totem and Taboo* [publishing information cited in following footnote] where Freud discusses projection in terms of the ambivalence of the father/son's love/hate relationship—succinctly, the sons (as members of a "brother band") kill the "primal" father but then blame his hostile impulses for their usurping actions, believing he forced them to act in such a manner. To relieve their psychic pain, they consume the father in a form of "communion" in an effort to reunite with him.

[42] Freud, *Totem and Taboo,* in *The Basic Writings of Sigmund Freud,* ed. and trans. A. A. Brill (NY: The Modern Library, 1938), renewed 1966, 855-56.

[43] Freud, *The Interpretation of Dreams*, 341.

[44] Whenever thinking about elaboration, I am somehow reminded of Rene Magritte's "The Treachery of Images," a realistic portrayal of a pipe—under which Magritte wrote, *"Ceci n'est pas une pipe"* (This is not a pipe) to awaken us to the conscious reality of what we are viewing, so we are not fooled by its symbolic representation.

[45] Peter Gay, *Freud: A Life for Our Time* (NY: W. W. Norton, 1998), 104.

[46] The objective psyche has come to be popularly known as the "collective unconscious" and will be subsequently referred to as such in this work.

[47] James A. Hall, M.D., *Jungian Dream Interpretation: A Handbook of Theory and Practice* (Toronto, Canada: Inner City Books, 1983), 9.

[48] Carl Gustav Jung, *Psyche & Symbol: A Selection from the Writings of C. G. Jung.* Violet S. de Laszlo, ed. (NY: Doubleday, 1958), 6.

[49] Jung, *Psyche & Symbol*, 6.

[50] M. –L. von Franz, "The Process of Individuation," in Carl G. Jung, *Man and his Symbols* (NY: Anchor Press, Doubleday, 1964), 160.

[51] Calvin S. Hall and Vernon J. Norby, *A Primer of Jungian Psychology* (Canada: Mentor Books, 1973), 81-82.

[52] Hall and Norby, 82.

[53] Hall and Nordby, 83.

[54] Hall and Nordby, 83.

[55] As he does, for example, in *The Red Book* (written over the period of 1914-1930 but not published until 2009 due to opposition from his family).

[56] Carl Gustav Jung, *Memories, Dreams, Reflections*, Aniela Jaffe, ed., trans. Richard and Clara Winston (NY: Random House, Vintage Books Edition, 1989).

[57] Carl Gustav Jung, *The Archetypes and the Collective Unconscious*, R.F.C. Hull, trans. Bollingen Series XX, 10th ed. (NY: Princeton University Press, 1990), 49.

[58] Carl Gustav Jung, *The Archetypes and the Collective Unconscious,* 49.

[59] Most likely from the Greek *prosopon* meaning face or mask, later popularized in its Latin form to refer to the masks actors wore in theatrical performances or to the roles adopted by participants in legal proceedings.

[60] Hall, 72.

[61] Hall, 73.

[62] Jung, *Psyche & Symbol*, 7.

[63] Jung, *Psyche & Symbol*, 7.

⁶⁴ Hall, 73-74.

⁶⁵ Hall and Nordby, 34.

⁶⁶ Hall and Nordby, 34-35.

⁶⁷ Jung, *Psyche & Symbol,* 12.

⁶⁸ Jung, *Psyche & Symbol, 12.*

⁶⁹ Robert Bly, *A Little Book on the Human Shadow,* William Booth, ed. (NY: HarperOne, Imprint of HarperCollins, 1988), 20-21.

⁷⁰ Hall, 74.

⁷¹ Hall, 74-75.

⁷² Jung, *Dreams*, first Princeton/Bollingen paperback ed., trans. R. F. C. Hull (Princeton, NJ: Princeton University Press, 174), 78.

⁷³ A spiritual *dojo*, a type of Buddhist meditation hall.

⁷⁴ Frederick S. Perls, *Gestalt Therapy Verbatim* (Utah: Real People Press, 1969), 2.

⁷⁵ Philip Brownell, *Gestalt Therapy: A Guide to Contemporary Practice* (NY: Springer Publishing, 2010), p. 170.

⁷⁶ Just as a director must be aware of all the visible elements in any frame of the movie, its *mise en scene,* gestalt analysis requires the analysand to recognize the juxtaposition of all facets composing the fore- and background of a dream.

⁷⁷ Talia Levine Bar-Yoseph and Jay Levin, "Gestalt in the New Age," in *Gestalt Therapy: Advances in Theory and Practice,* Talia Levine Bar-Yoseph, ed. (NY: Routledge, 2012), 7.

⁷⁸ Perls, 217.

⁷⁹ Perls, 3-4.

⁸⁰ *Dasein* can be literally translated as "being-there" and refers to human existence in both waking and sleeping life as opposed to the psychic approach of psychoanalysis.

⁸¹ Medard Boss, *I Dreamt Last Night: a New Approach to the Revelations of Dreaming—and its uses in Psychotherapy* (NY: Gardner Press, 1977), 24.

[82] Boss, *I Dreamt Last Night,* 214.

[83] Medard Boss, *The Analysis of Dreams*, trans. Arnold J. Pomerans (NY: Philosophical Library, Inc., 1958), 53.

[84] Rodolphe Kasser, et al., eds. *The Gospel of Judas from Codex Tchacos* (Washington, DC: National Geographic Society, 2006), intro.2.

[85] Delaney, *All About Dreams,* 85.

[86] Anna Freud, *The Ego and the Mechanisms of Defense*, revised ed. (Madison, CT: International Universities Press, 1966), 16.

[87] Alan B. Siegel, "Children's Dreams and Nightmares: Emerging Trends in Research," *Dreaming: Journal of the Association for the Study of Dreams* 15.3 (September 2005): 153.

[88] Chronicled in Anna Freud and Dorothy T. Burlingham, *War and Children*, orig. pub. Medical War Books, 1943 (NY: Ernst Willard, 1943).

[89] Anna Freud, "Indications for Child Analysis (1945)" in *The Psychoanalytical Treatment of Children: Lectures and Essays* (NY: Schocken Books, 1964), 81-82.

[90] Anna Freud, *Introduction to the Technic of Child Analysis,* Classics in Child Development edition (NY: Arno Press, 1975), 19.

[91]Anna Freud, *Introduction to the Technic of Child Analysis,* 19-20.

[92] Anna Freud, *Introduction to the Technic of Child Analysis,* 20-21.

[93] Anna Freud, *Introduction to the Technic of Child Analysis,* 21-22.

[94] Melanie Klein, *Love, Guilt and Reparation & Other Works* (NY: Delta Books, 1975),146.

[95] Melanie Klein, *The Psychoanalysis of Children*, trans. Alix Strachey, revised ed. (NY: Delta Books, 1975), 7-8.

[96] Klein, *Love, Guilt and Reparation,* 147.

[97] Klein, *Love, Guilt, and Reparation,* 147.

[98] Klein, *The Psychoanalysis of Children,* 18.

[99] Klein, *The Psychoanalysis of Children, 18.*

[100] Montague Ullman, "Basic Dream Work—An Objective Comparison of Dream Groups & Therapy." *Dream Network Journal of the Exploration of Dreams* 9.1 (Winter, 1990): n.p.

[101] Ullman, "Basic Dream Work," n.p.

[102] Montague Ullman, "Dream, Metaphor and Psi," in R. A. White and R. S. Brougton, eds. *Research in Parapsychology* (Metuchen, NJ: Scarecrow Press, 1983), 140.

[103] Montague Ullman, Stanley Krippner, and Allan Vaughan, *Dream Telepathy* (NY: Macmillan Publishing, 1973), 41.

[104] Ullman, "Dream, Metaphor, and Psi," 143.

[105] Ullman, "Dream, Metaphor, and Psi," P. 144.

[106] Ullman, "Dream, Metaphor, and Psi," 150.

[107] Ullman, "Dreams, Metaphor, and Psi," 151.

[108] Ullman, "Dream Work and the General Public," from paper presented at The Association for the Study of Dreams Conference III, June 23-29, 1986. Ottawa, Ontario, Canada.

[109] Anna O is the name given to Josef Breuer's patient, Bertha Pappenheim, to protect her identity. Due to his countertransference, Breuer referred Bertha to Sigmund Freud.

[110] There is a saying in psychoanalysis that "the transference is all." It is only when an analysand turns the analyst into the person who originally caused the emotion trauma does real therapy begin.

[111] Ole Vedfelt, *The Dimensions of Dreams: From Freud and Jung to Boss, Perls, and REM, a Comprehensive Scourcebook*, trans. Kenneth Tindall (NY: Fromm International, 1998), 288.

[112] Vedfelt, 290.

[113] Vedfelt, 292.

[114] Vedfelt, 291.

[115] Hyman Spotnitz, *Modern Psychoanalysis of the Schizophrenic Patient: Theory of the Technique,* 2nd ed. (NY: Human Sciences Press, 1985), 35.

[116] Joining techniques include but are not limited to ego syntonic responses, in which the analysand will respond with only the most benign comments, and ego-dystonic

responses, in which the analyst challenges the analysand to facilitate the discharge of negative effects.

[117] Spotnitz, 182.

[118] Spotnitz, 152.

[119] Spotnitz, 167.

[120] Spotnitz, 286.

[121] Spotnitz, 171.

[122] Spotnitz, 172.

[123] Spotnitz, ibid.

[124] Delaney, *All About Dreams,* 1.

[125] Delaney, *All About Dreams,* 3.

[126] Delaney, *All About Dreams,* 4.

[127] Delaney, *All About Dreams,* 103.

[128] Delaney, *All About Dreams,* 103-104.

[129] Delaney, *All About Dreams,* 105.

[130] Delaney, telephone interview by author, 10 June 2014.

[131] Delaney, *All About Dreams,* 204-209.

[132] Delaney, *All About Dreams,* 7.

[133] As Hamlet assures Horatio, there is indeed more to heaven and earth than our philosophies.

[134] William Wordsworth, "Intimations of Immortality" in *Poems in Two Volumes,* vol. 2 (1807). Web. Amazon Digital Book Series (March 23, 2011). Kindle, n.p.

[135] Jung, *Man and His Symbols,* 52.

[136] Qtd. in Michael Tucker, *Dreaming with Open Eyes: The Shamanic Spirit in Twentieth Century Art and Culture* (Hammersmith, London: Aquarian/Thorsons, imprint of HarperCollins, 1992), 7.

[137] Christopher Kemp, "Walking with Cavemen," *New Scientist* , 220, 2948 (21 December 2013), p. 66.

[138] William Shakespeare, *The Tempest, The Complete Works of Shakespeare*, 5th ed. Bevington, David, ed. (NY: Pearson-Langham, 2003), 1597.

[139] Very little is known about the life of Zhuangzi (Master Zhuang) other than a brief mention in Sima Qion's *Records of the Grand Historian.*

[140] Marc Ian Barasch, *Healing Dreams: Exploring the Dreams that Can Transform Your Life* (NY: Riverhead Books, Penguin Putnam, 2000), 307-308.

[141] Carl Gustav Jung, "The Meaning of Psychology for Modern Man," *Civilization in Transition, CWJ*, X (Princeton, NJ: Princeton University Press, 1970), par. 304-05.

[142] Shakespeare, *Hamlet, Bevington,* 1119.

[143] Alison George, "Are You Thinking What I'm Thinking…," *New Scientist* 220, no. 2944 (23 November 2013), 38.

[144] A Chinese philosophical/medicinal epiphany of the universal life force or energy that informs and instructs the body and is in all living things.

[145] Jung, *Man and His Symbols*, 98.

[146] Marija Gimbutas, *The Language of the Goddess* (San Francsico, CA: HarperSanFrancisco, 1989): introduction, xv.

[147] William Wordsworth, "The World is Too Much With Us," in *Poems in Two Volumes,* vol. 2 (1807). Web. Amazon Digital Book Series (March 23, 2011). Kindle, n.p.

[148] Alexander Marshack, *The Roots of Civilization* { NY: Moyer Bell, 1991), 44-48.

[149] Humans actually have three separate brains—innermost is the reptilian core, which is covered over by the paleomammalian (or old mammal) brain, which is itself encircled by the neomammalian (or new mammal) brain.

[150] Rather than perceived as a phallus, it was understood to be the "wandering womb" of the Goddess.

[151] Although later Greek writing portrays the Python as male, the earliest accounts identify it as female.

[152] Merlin Stone, *When God Was a Woman* (NY: Harcourt Brace, 1976), 203.

153 Stone, 210.

154 Stone, 213-14.

155 Robert A. Wilcox and Emma M. Whitham, "The Symbol of Modern Medicine: Why One Snake is More than Two," *Annals of Internal Medicine,* Philadelphia, 238, no. 8 (Apr. 15, 2003), web.

156 Alchemists were referred to as sons of Hermes and deemed Hermetists or Hemeticists.

157 Keith Blayney, "The Caduceus vs. the Staff of Asclepius (Aklepian)" (Sept. 2002, revised Oct. 2005) electronic article.

158 Along with the staff of Asclepius, which was also used.

159 Qtd. in Wilcox and Whitman.

160 Qtd. in Wilcox and Whitman.

161 Blaney.

162 Wilcox and Whitman.

163 This is true even today, as evidenced by the recognition that "in every medicine is a little bit of poison."

164 The Goddess as vehicle of resurrection is discussed later in this chapter.

165 Christopher Lawrence, "The Healing Serpent—The Snake in Medical Iconography." The Sir Thomas and Lady Dixon Memorial Lecture, posted on *PubMed Central*, online journal of U.S. National Institutes of Health 47.2 (1978): 135.

166 Lawrence, 134.

167Lawrence, 140.

168 Brain structure overlaps in the sense that there are men whose brains have more feminine structures and females whose brains have more masculine structures than the generalization.

169 Francesco Aristide Ancona, *Femina Sapiens: A Study of Women Through Imagery: The First Truly Thinking Human Beings* (Ohio: The Rhodes-Fulbright Library, Wyndham Hall Press, 2005).

170 The language of prehistoric art can be understood by recognizing how 00001analogical it is and realizing that many of the epiphanies, especially regarding the

Goddess, pregnancy and menstruation, must have come from women as, even today, men are either not comfortable or unable to discuss such issues.

[171] For an comprehensive examination of Goddess shapes and forms in prehistoric art, see Marija Gimbutas, *The Language of the Goddess* (San Francisco, CA: HarperSanFrancisco, 1989).

[173] This seems to be a prehistoric idea emergent at the birth of history by Dionysius as grape of the vine and echoed through these words of the "Hail Mary": "And blessed is the fruit of thy womb, Jesus."

[174] Please note the numerous spiritual rebirths expressed through tree imagery: Christ is resurrected on a wooden cross; Odin sacrifices "himself to himself" to be recreated on Yggdrasil; and the Buddha awakens to nirvana under the Bodhi tree.

[175] Please see Chapter One, the section on nightmares.

[176] Ancona, *Femina Sapiens,* 8.

[177] Ancona, *Femina Sapiens,* 9.

[178] Ancona, *Femina Sapiens,* 112.

[179] Riane Eisler, *The Chalice and the Blade: Our History, Our Future* (San Francisco, CA: Harper & Rowe, 1987), 2.

[180] Note how, in contrast during historical times, the bull imagery is connected to the male, as in the bull tail worn by Egyptian Pharaohs or their worship of the Apis bull or, more notably in Zeus' adoption of a bull form to rape and abandon the Phoenician princess Europa, who—interestingly enough—had a premonition of her fate in a dream.

[181] Gimbutas, 265-66.

[182] Perhaps, this could also be a prehistoric intuition that all fetuses are initially female. If so, the shaman's dream-trance becomes a journey to achieve apotheosis with the Goddess.

[183] Marija Gimbutas discusses the various aspects of Goddess Bird imagery in chapters four, nine, and nineteen of *The Language of the Goddess.*

[184] Leonard Shlain, *The Alphabet Versus the Goddess: The Conflict Between Word and Image* (NY: Viking, 1998): 7.

[185] Theresa Betherat and Carol Berstein, *The Body Has Its Reasons* (VT: Inner Tradition, 1989),
48.

186 Schlain, 39.

187 To illustrate, images of war among prehistoric Goddess cults are rare if even existent; whereas, the historical, male deity dominated era is inundated with war and dominance.

188 Hughes.

189 Hughes.

190 Christopher Lawrence, 134.

191 Lawrence, 134.

192 Brenner, 92.

193 Paula A. Nielson, "The Rod of Asclepius and the Caduceus Symbols: Ancient Greek Snake Symbolism of Healing and Medicine" (March 16, 2010). Online posting. Web., n.p.

194 Delaney, *All About Dreams*, 15.

195 Hughes.

196 Ogden Goelet, Jr., commentary in *The Egyptian Book of the Dead: The Book of Going Forth by Day*, Raymond Faulkner, trans. San Francisco: Chronicle Books, 1998: 142.

197 Goelet, 150.

198 Nathan W. Williams, "Greek ASKLEPIOS, Latin AESCULAPIUS (or Asculapius) Roman God of Medicine," *JAMA*, 281 (1999), 475.

199 Audrey Cruse, *Roman Medicine* (Gloucestershire: Tempus, 2004), 31.

200 Gimbutas, 31.

201 Gimbutas, 75.

202 Carla Barbe, "Ancient Theories About Dreams," Web manuscript, Academia.edu, n.d., n.p., downloaded 26 June 2014.

203 Paul Carrick, *Medical Ethics in the Ancient World* (Washington, D.C.: Georgetown University Press, 2001, 18.

204 Pieter Willem van der Horst, ed. *Persuasion and Dissuasion in Early Chritianity, Ancient Judaism, and Hellenism.* Leuven, Belgium: Peeters Publishing, 2003, 88.

205 Delaney, *All About Dreams,* 17-18.

206 Delaney, *All About Dreams,* 18.

207 Carla Barbe.

208 Walter Brueggemann, "The Power of Dreams in the Bible," in *The Christian Century,* the Christian Century Foundation (June 28, 2005) 28-31. Web. Academia.edu. Religion online.

209 Qtd. in Lldiko Csepregi, "Mysteries for the Uninitiated: The Role and Symbolism of the Eucharist in Miraculous Dream Healing," in the *Eucharist in Theology and Philosophy: Issues of Doctrinal History in the East and West from the Patristic Age to the Reformation,* eds. L. Perczel, R. Forrai, G. Gereby (Leuven: Leuven University Press, 2006): 97-130. Web. Academic Education online.

210 Lldiko Csepregi.

211 Lldiko Csepregi.

212 Delaney, *All About Dreams,* 28.

213 Roberto Keh Ong, *The Interpretation of Dreams in Ancient China*, Masters of Art Thesis, University of British Columbia in Retrospective Theses and Dissertations, 1919-2007 collection, Vancouver, B.C. (May, 1981): 19.

214 Roberto Keh Ong, 45.

215Roberto Keh Ong, 46-47.

216 Joseph Campbell, *The Mythic Image*, Bollingen Series C., (Princeton, NJ: Princeton University Press, 1981), xi.

217 Joseph Campbell, *The Mythic Image,* 361.

218 Joseph Campbell, *The Mythic Image,* 362.

219 Joseph Campbell, *Historical Atlas of World Mythology, vol. I, part 2: The Way of the Animal Powers, part 2: Mythologies of the Great Hunt* (Cambridge: Harper & Row, Perennial Library, 1988), 138.

220 Campbell, *Historical Atlas of World Mythology, vol. 1, part 2,* 141.

[221] Please see the Hindu epic, *Mahabharata,* which narrates their mythology.

[222] Francesco Aristide Ancona, *Myth: Matter of Mind?* (Lanham, MD: University Press of America, 1994): 5.

[223] A Buddhist reference to AUM can be recognized in the question:" What is the sound of one hand clapping?"

[224] Heinrich Zimmer, *The Art of Indian Asia, vol. 1,* ed. Joseph Campbell, Bollingen Series XXXIX (Princeton, NJ: Princeton University Press, 1983), 123.

[225] Reminiscent of the dancing sorcerer of *Les Trois Freres.*

[226] Joseph Campbell, *The Mythic Image,* 359.

[227] Lilith's appearance can be traced to at least early Babylonian Talmudic times.

[228] Joseph Campbell, *The Mythic Image,* 359.

[229] The name Siddhartha supports the proposition that his desire for *nirvana* is just this, a desire, and it is one motivated by the fear of entrapment in the life and death cyclical realm of *samsara.*

[230] Qtd. in Francisco J. Varela, narrator and editor, *Sleeping, Dreaming, and Dying: An Exploration of Consciousness with the Dalai Lama* (Boston: Wisdom Publications, 1997): 111.

[231] Qtd. in Francisco J. Varela, 111 -112.

[232] Roxanne Struthers, "The Lived Experience of Ojibwa and Cree Women Healers, *Journal of Holistic Nursing* 18.3 (September 2000): 275.

[233] Roxanne Struthers, 269.

[234] Contrast the Native American "reclaiming" of this nurturing image with the negative, fearful associations cast by contemporary American culture.

[235] Vine Deloria, Jr., *The World We Used to Live In* (CO: Fulcrum Publishing, 2006): 16-17.

[236] Vine Deloria, Jr., 17.

[237] Joseph Campbell with Bill Moyers, *The Power of Myth,* Betty Sue Flowers, ed. (NY: Doubleday, 1988): 88-89.

[238] Perhaps suggesting a primitive evolutionary origin of hypnogogic and hypnopompic states from crepuscular creatures like bats and insects?

[239] Deloria, Jr., 8-9.

[240] Russell E. Phillips III and Kenneth I. Pargament, "The Sanctification of Dreams: Prevalence and Implications ," *Dreaming: Journal of the Association for the Study of Dreams* 12.3 (September 2002): 141.

[241] Phillips and Pargament, 146.

[242] Don Kuiken, Ming-Ni Lee, Tracy Eng, and Terry Singh, "The Influence of Impactful Dreams on Self-Perceptual Depth and Spiritual Transformation," *Dreams: Journal of the Association for the Study of Dreams,* 16.4 (December 2006): 258.

[243] Fred R. Gustafson, *Dancing Between Two Worlds: Jung and the Native American Soul* (NY: Paulist Press, 1997): 35-36.

[244] Gustafson, 36.

[245] It is my belief that the loss of soul in matter is the reason so many youths are seeking escape through immersion in alternative realities, such as video games and fantasy role playing.

[246] Phillips and Pargament, 151.

[247] Phillips and Pargament, 152.

[248] Atoms are composed of protons, neutrons, and electrons.

[249] A phrase that has become part of popular culture culled from a speech by Winston Churchill on understanding Russia.

[250] Meredith Sabini, "Dreams: In Sickness and in Health," *Dreamtime,* Publication of the International Association for the Study of Dreams, 30.2 (Spring 2013): 6.

[251] Carl Gustav Jung, *Jung: Analytical Psychology*, 1st pub. GB 1968, paperback ed. (NY: Routledge, 2014): 53.

[252] Sabini, 36.

[253] Stewart Means, "Ancient Healing and the Modern Mind," *The Journal of Religion,* 5.1 (Jan. 1925): 73.

[254] Means, 73-74.

255 Harry Hoffner, Jr. "Ancient Views of Prophecy and Fulfillment: Mesopotamia and Asia Minor," *JETS* 30.3 (September 1987): 261.

256 Hoffner, 261.

257 Hoffner, 261-262.

258 Gayle Delaney, *All About Dreams: Everything You Need to Know About Why We Have Them, What They Mean, and How to Put Them to Work for You* (CA: HarperSanFrancisco, 1998): 16.

259 Jackson Steward Lincoln, *The Dream in Primitive Cultures*, first ed. 1935 (NY: Johnson Reprint Corporation, 1970): 4.

260 Lincoln, 4.

261 James McClenon, "Shamanic Healing, Human Evolution, and the Origin of Religions, *Journal for the Scientific Study of Religion,* 36.3 (1997): 345.

262 The Egyptian symbol for dream, drawn as an open eye, is *rswt*, the root of which refers to a state of awakening. Like dreams, death was not an end; rather, it was an awakening to a new dream.

263 William Shakespeare, *Hamlet, Prince of Denmark*, in *The Complete Works of William Shakespeare,* 5th ed., David Bevington, editor (NJ: Pearson Education, 2004): 1119.

264 Ogen Goelet, commentary in *The Egyptian Book of the Dead: The Book of Going Forth by Day*, Raymond D. Faulkner, trans., Ogen Goelet, additional trans., ed. Eva von Dassow (CA: Chronicle Books, 1998): 15.

265 Jeffrey B. Pettis, "Earth, Dream, and Healing: The Integration of *Materia* and Psyche in the Ancient World," *Journal of Religion and Health,* 45.1 (spring 2006): 120.

266 Delaney, 33.

267 Lee T. Pearcy, "Dreams in Ancient Medicine," *Medicina Antiqua*, Wellcome [sic] Trust Centre for the History of Medicine at UCL, London, n.d.. Web.

268 Louise Cilliers and Francois Pieter Retief, "Dream Healing in Asclepieia in the Mediterranean," *Dreams, Healing, and Medicine in Greece: From Antiquity to the Present,* Stephen M. Oberhelman, ed. (England: Ashgate Publishing, Ltd.,m 2013): 69.

269 Pearcy.

270 *Oneiron* is the Greek word for dreams.

[271] Christine Walde, "Illness and Its Metaphors in Artemidorus' *Oneirocritica: A Negative List*," in *Dreams, Healing, and Medicine in Greece: from Antiquity to the Present*, Steven M. Oberhelman, ed. (England: Ashgate Publishing, Ltd., 2013): 129.

[272] Walde, 137.

[273] Walde, 138.

[274] Walde, 151.

[275] Pettis, 115.

[276] Pettis, 116.

[277] Pettis, 117.

[278] Johnston-Saint, "An Outline of the History of Medicine in India, *Journal of the Royal Society of Arts,* 77.3999 (July 12th, 1929): 856.

[279] Johnston-Saint, 864-865.

[280] Johnston-Saint, 867.

[281] Johnston-Saint, 868.

[282] Alex Wayman, "Significance of Dreams in India and Tibet," *History of Religions,* 7.1. (Aug. 1967): 3.

[283] Cited in Wayman, 4.

[284] Wayman, 4.

[285] Wayman, 10.

[286] A sacred Hindu text written circa 1200-1000 B.C.E. by rishis (poet-seers who communicated with the gods through their verses), often called the "fourth *Veda*" of the four *Vedas*.

[287] Wayan, 6.

[288] Lincoln, 68-69.

[289] Howard Giskin, "Dreaming the Seven-Colored Flower: Eastern and Western Approaches to Dreams in Chinese Folk Literature," Nanzan University, *Asian Folklore Studies,* 63.1 (2004): 80.

[290] Giskin, 81.

291 Giskin, 82.

292 Giskin, 84.

293 Giskin, 84.

294 This "hero/heroine" is within each of us and is not to be recognized as some separate, special "other."

295 Giskin, 85.

296 Hsiu-fen Chen, "Between Passion and Repression: Medical Views of Demon Dreams, Demonic Fetuses, and Female Sexual Madness in Late Imperial China," Society for Qing Studies and the Johns Hopkins University Press, *Late Imperial China* 32.1 (June 2011): 59.

297 Hysteria—from the Greek *hystera*, "uterus"—often manifested as physical ailments of the body.

298 Hsiu-fen Chen, 51.

299 Hsiu-fen Chen, 66-67.

300 Hsiu-fen Chen, 69.

301 Lee Irwin, "Cherokee Healing: Myth, Dreams, and Medicine," *American Indian Quarterly,* 16.2 (Spring 1992): 244.

302 Irwin, 244.

303 Irwin, 247.

304 Irwin, 247.

305 Lincoln, 249.

306 Tom Lowenstein and Piers Vitebsky, *Mother Earth, Father Sky: Native American Myth*, in *Myth and Mankind* series (London: Duncan Baird Publishers, 1997): 114.

307 The Goddess tradition is discussed in Chapter Four.

308 Barbara Tedlock, "The Role of Dreams and Visionary Narratives in Mayan Cultural Survival," *Ethos*, 20.4 (December, 1992): 455-456.

309 Tedlock, "The Role of Dreams and Visionary Narratives in Mayan Cultural Survival," 456.

310 Tedlock, "The Role of Dreams and Visionary Narratives in Mayan Cultural Survival," 467.

311 Barbara Tedlock, "Divination as a Way of Knowing: Embodiment, Visualisation, Narrative, and Interpretation," *Folklore,* 112.2 (October, 2001): 192.

312 Tedlock, "Divination as a Way of Knowing: Embodiment, Visualisation, Narrative, and Interpretation," 192.

313 Philip Hunter, "To Sleep, Perchance to Live: Sleeping is Vital for Health, Cognitive Function, Memory, and Long Life," *European Molecular Biology Organization Reports,* 9.11 (November 2008): 1070.

314 Hunter, 1071-1072.

315 Hunter, 1072.

316 Sarah Mednick, in *What are Dreams? Inside the Sleeping Brain.* Nova documentary. Jamie Effros, et al. Colville, Charles and Sarah Holt, directors. PBS Productions, 2009.

317 A discussion of REM and non-REM dream states follows below in this chapter.

318 Hunter, 1072.

319 Robert Stickgold, in *What are Dreams? Inside the Sleeping Brain.* Nova documentary. Jamie Effros, et al. Colville, Charles and Sarah Holt, directors. PBS Productions, 2009.

320 M.C. Lopes, M.A. Quera-Salva, and C. Guilleminault, "Non-REM Sleep Instability in Patients with Major Depressive Disorder: Subjective Improvement of Non-REM Sleep Instability with Treatment (Agomelatine)," *Sleep Medicine,* 1 (December 9, 2007): n.p. Web. PubMed.Gov, U.S. National Library of Medicine, National Institutes of Health.

321 C. Guilleminault, C. Kirisogluc, A.C. daRosa, C. Lopes, and A. Chan, "Sleepwalking, a Disorder of NREM Sleep Instability," *Sleep Medicine,* 2 (March 7, 2006): n.p. Epub. February 3, 2006. Web. PubMed.Gove, U.S. National Library of Medicine, National Institutes of Health.

322 William Shakespeare, *A Midsummer Night's Dream,* in *The Complete Works of Shakespeare,* 5th ed., David Bevington, editor (NY: Pearson, Longman, 2003), 173.

323 Tom Holm, *Strong Hearts and Wounded Souls: Native American Veterns of the Vietnam War* (Texas: University of Texas Press, Austin, 1996): 169.

324 Holm, 168-69.

325 Jan Roberts, C. J. Lennings and R. Heard, "Nightmares, Life Stress, and Anxiety: An Examination of Tension Reduction," *Dreaming, Journal of the Association for the Study of Dreams,* 19.1 (March 2009): 17-18.

326 Dante Picchioni, et al., "Nightmares as a Coping Mechanism for Stress," *Dreaming: Journal of the Association for the Study of Dreams,* 12.3 (September 2002): 167.

327 Antii Revonsuo, *What are Dreams? Inside the Sleeping Brain,* Nova documentary, Jamie Effros, et al. Charles Colville and Sarah Holt, directors. PBS Productions, 2009.

328 Desmond Morris, *The Naked Ape,* 5th edition (NY: Dell Publishing, 1969): 192-193.

329 Revonsuo, *What are Dreams?*

330 J. A. Cheyne, "Sleep Parlysis and the Structure of Waking-Nightmare Hallucinations," *Dreaming: Journal of the Association for the Study of Dreams,* 13.3 (September 2003): 177.

331 Edward F. Pace-Schott, "The Neurobiology of Dreaming," in *Principles and Practice of Sleep Medicine, 5th ed.,* Meir H. Kryger, T. Roth, and William C. Dement, eds. (Canada: Elsevier, 2011): 568.

332 Cheyne, 176.

333 Pace-Schott, 567.

334 Thomas A. Mellman and Wilfred R. Pigeon, "Dreams and Nightmares in Posttraumatic Stress Disorder," in *Principles and Practice of Sleep Medicaine.* Kryger, Roth, and Dement, eds. (Canada: Elsevier, 2011): 616.

335 Mellman and Pigeon, 614.

336 Mellman and Pigeon, 614.

337 Mellman and Pigeon, 613.

338 Mellman and Pigeon, 613.

³³⁹ "PTSD: National Center for PTSD," U. S. Department of Veterans Affairs. Web. 26 August 2014. Retrieved 19 September 2014.

³⁴⁰ "Drugs and Supplements: Prazosin," Mayo Clinic, Mayo Foundation for Medical Education and Research. Web. 2014. Retrieved 20 September 2014.

³⁴¹ Mellman and Pigeon, 613.

³⁴² Anne Germain, et al., "Increased Mastery Elements Associated with Imagery Rehearsal Treatment for Nightmares in Sexual Assault Survivors with PTSD," *Dreaming: Journal of the Association for the Study of Dreams* 14.4 (December 2004): 196.

³⁴³ Germain, et al., 204.

³⁴⁴ Brigitte Holzinger, Stephen LaBerge, and Lynne Levitan, "Psychophysiological Correlates of Lucid Dreaming," *Dreaming: Journal of the Association for the Study of Dreams*, 16.2 (June 2006): 88.

³⁴⁵ Holzinger, LaBerge, and Levitan.

³⁴⁶ William Shakespeare, *Hamlet,* in *The Complete Works of Shakespeare,* 5th edition, David Bevington, editor (NY: Pearson/Longman, 2004): 1119.

³⁴⁷ William Shakespeare, *Macbeth,* in *The Complete Works of Shakespeare,* 5th edition, David Bevington, editor (NY: Pearson Longman, 2004): 1269.

³⁴⁸ Donald L. Bliwise, "Normal Aging," in *Principles and Practice of Sleep Medicine.* Kryger, Roth, and Dement, eds. (Canada: Elsevier, 2011): 27.

³⁴⁹ James K. Walsh, William C. Dement, and David F. Dinges, "Sleep Medicine, Public Policy, and Public Health," in *Principles and Practice of Sleep Medicine.* Kryger, Roth, and Dement, eds. (Canada: Elsevier, 2011): 722.

³⁵⁰ Walsh, Dement, and Dinges, 721.

³⁵¹ Michael J. Lowis, "Dreams and Their Relation to Physical and Mental Well-being," *The Journal of Social, Political, and Economic Studies,* 35.3 (Fall 21010): 366.

³⁵² Lowis, 377-78.

³⁵³ Soledad Coo, Jeannette Milgrom, and John Trinder, "Pregnancy and Postnatal Dreams Reflect Changes to the Transition to Motherhood," *Dreaming: Journal of the Association for the Study of Dreams,* 24.2 (June 2014): 125.

³⁵⁴ Coo, Milgrom, and Trinder, 125.

[355] Roger M. Knudson, "Anorexia Dreaming" A Case Study," *Dreaming: Journal of the Association for the Study of Dreams,* 16.1 (March 2006):50.

[356] Knudson, 50.

[357] Leland van den Daele, "Direct Interpretation of Dreams: Neuropsychology," *American Journal of Psychoanalysis*, 56.3 (September 1996): 265-66.

[358] Lulu Xie, et al., "Sleep Drives Metabolite Clearance from the Adult Brain," *Science* 342 (2013): 373.

[359] Xie, et al., 373.

[360] Xie, et al., 373.

[361] Xie, et al., 376-77.

[362] Walsh, Dement, Dinges, 718.

[363] Shahrokh Javaheri, "Sleep and Cardiovascular Disease: Present and Future," *Principles and Practice of Sleep Medicine.* Kryger, Roth, and Dement, eds. (Canada: Elsevier, 2011): 1349-50.

[364] Ronald Grunstein, "Endocrine Disorders,"*Principles and Practice of Sleep Medicine.* Kryger, Roth, and Dement, eds. (Canada: Elsevier, 2011): 1435.

[365] Richard L. Verrier and Murray A. Mittleman, "Sleep-Related Cardiac Risk," *Principles and Practice of Sleep Medicine.* Kryger, Roth, and Dement, eds. (Canada: Elsevier, 2011): 1353.

[366] Sonia Ancoli-Israel and Josee Savard, "Sleep and Fatigue in Cancer Patients," *Principles and Practice of Sleep Medicine.* Kryger, Roth, and Dement, eds. (Canada: Elsevier, 2011): 1416.

[367] James G. MacFarlance and Harvey Moldofsky, "Fibromyalgia and Chronic Fatigue Syndromes," *Principles and Practice of Sleep Medicine.* Kryger, Roth, and Dement, eds. (Canada: Elsevier, 2011): 1422.

[368] Jan Van den Bulck, "Media Use and Dreaming: The Relationship Among Television Viewing, Computer Game Play, and Nightmares or Pleasant Dreams," *Dreaming: Journal of the Association for the Study of Dreams*, 14.1 (March 2004): 43.

[369] Van den Bulck, 48.

³⁷⁰ Jayne Gackenbach, "Electronic Media and Lucid-Control Dreams: Morning After Reports," *Dreaming: Journal of the Association for the Study of Dreams*, 19.1 (March 2009): 1.

³⁷¹ Jayne Gackenbach, "Video Game Play and Lucid Dreams: Implications for the Development of Consciousness," 16.2 *Dreaming: Journal of the Association for the Study of Dreams,* 16.2 (June 2006): 96.

³⁷² Gackenbach, "Video Game Play and Lucid Dreams: Implications for the Development of Consciousness," 109.

³⁷³ Jayne Gackenbach and Arielle Boyes, "Social Media Versus Gaming Associations with Typical and Recent Dreams," *Dreaming: Journal of the Association for the Study of Dreams*, 24.3 (September 2014): 182.

³⁷⁴ Shinji Nishimoto, et al., "Reconstructing Visual Experiences from Brain Activity Evoked by Natural Movies," *Current Biology* 21.19 (October 11, 2011): 1641.

³⁷⁵ Jean Thilmany, "Next-Day Dreams," *Mechanical Engineering,* 134.3 (March 2012): 18.

REFERENCES

Ancoli-Israel and Josee Savard. "Sleep and Fatigue in Cancer Patients." *Principles and Practice of Sleep Medicine.* Edited by Kryger, Roth, and Dement. Canada:Elsevier, 2011: 1416-21.

Ancona, Francesco Aristide. *Femina Sapiens: A Study of Women Through Imagery: The First Truly Thinking Human Beings.* Ohio: Wyndham Hall Press, 2005.

------. *Myth: Matter of Mind?* NY: University Press of America, 1994.

Barbe, Carla. "Ancient Theories About Dreams." Academia.edu. http://www.academia.edu/ 3100958/Ancient_Theories_ about_Dreams (accessed 26 June 2014).

Barasch, Marc Ian. *Healing Dreams: Exploring the Dreams that can Transform Your Life.* NY: Riverhead, Penguin, 2000.

Betherat, Theresa and Carol Berstein. *The Body has Its Reasons.* VT: Inner Tradition, 1989.

Blayney, Keith. "The Caduceus vs. the Staff of Asclepius (Aklepian)." Electronic article, September 2002, revised October 2005. http://www.drblayney.com/Asclepius.html (accessed 21 May 2014).

Bliwise, Donald. "Normal Aging." *Principles and Practice of Sleep Medicine.* Edited by Kryger, Roth, and Dement. Canada: Elsevier, 2011: 27-41.

Bly, Robert. *A little Book on the Human Shadow.* Edited by William Booth. NY: HarperOne, 1988.

Boss, Medard. *I Dreamt Last Night: a New Approach to the Revelations of Dreaming— and its uses in Psychotherapy.* NY: Gardner Press, 1977.

------. *The Analysis of Dreams.* Trans. Arnold J. Pomeranz. NY: Philosophical Library,Inc., 1958.

Brenner, Charles. *An Elementary Textbook of Psychoanalysis.* NY: Anchor Books, 1974.

Brownell, Philip. *Gestalt Therapy: A Guide to Contemporary Practice.* NY: Springer Publishing, 2010.

Brueggemann, Walter. "The Power of Dreams in the Bible." Christian Century Foundation. Academia.edu. http://www.religion-online.org/showarticle.acp?title=3218 (accessed 8 March 2014).

Campbell, Joseph. *The Hero with a Thousand Faces.* Bollingen Series, XVII. NJ: Princeton University Press, 1973.

------. *Historical Atlas of World Mythology, vol. 1: The Way of the Animal Powers, part 2: Mythologies of the Great Hunt.* Cambridge: Harper & Row, 1988.

------. *The Inner Reaches of Outer Space: Metaphor as Myth and as Religion.* NY:Perennial Library, Harper & Row, 1986.

Campbell, Joseph with Bill Moyers. *The Power of Myth.* Edited by Betty Sue Flowers.NY: Doubleday, 1988.

Carrick, Paul. *Medical Ethics in the Ancient World.* Washington, D.C.: Georgetown University Press, 2001.

Chen, Hsiu-fen. "Between Passion and Repression: Medical Views of Demon Dreams, Demonic Features, and Female Sexual Madness in Late Imperial China." *Late Imperial China* 32.1 (June 2011): 51-83.

Cheyne, J. A. "Sleep Paralysis and the Structure of Waking-Nightmare Hallucinations." *Dreaming: Journal of the Association for the Study of Dreams* 13.3 (September 2003): 163-180.

Cilliers, Louise and Frocois Pieter Retief, "Dream Healing in Asclepieia in the Mediterranean." *Dreams, Healing, and Medicine in Greece: From Antiquity to the Present.* Edited by Stephen M. Oberhelman. England: Ashgate Publishing, Ltd., 2013: 69-91.

Coo, Soledad, Jeannette Milgrom, and John Trinder. "Pregnancy and Postnatal Dreams Reflect Changes to the Transition to Motherhood." *Dreaming: Journal of the Association for the Study of Dreams* 24.2 (June 2014): 125-137.

Cruse, Audrey. *Roman Medicine.* Gloucestershire: Tempus Publishing, Ltd., 2004.

Csepregi, Lldiko. "Mysteries for the Uninitiated: The Role and Symbolism of the Eucharist in Miraculous Dream Healing." *Eucharist in Theology and Philosophy: Issues of Doctrinal History in the East and West from the Patristic Age to the Reformation.* Editied by L. Perczel, R. Forrai, and G. Gereby. Leuven: Leuven University Press, 2006: 97-130. http://www.academia.edu/445985/Symbolism_of _the Eucharist_in_Miraculous_Dream_Healing.

Delaney, Gayle. *All About Dreams: Everything You Need to Know About Why We Have Them, What They Mean, and How to Put Them to Work for You.* CA: Harper SanFrancisco, 1998.--------.Telephone interview by author, 10 June 2014.

Deloria, Vine, Jr. *The World We Used to Live In.* CO: Fulcrum Publishing, 2006."Drugs and Supplements: Prazosin." Mayo Clinic. Mayo Foundation for Medical

Education and Research, 2014. http://www.mayoclinic.org/drugs-supplements/prazosin-oral-route/description/drg-20065617 (accessed 20 September 2014).

Eisler, Riane. *The Chalice and the Blade: Our History, Our Future.* San Francisco, CA: Harper & Rowe, 1987.

Freud, Anna. *The Ego and the Mechanisms of Defense.* Madison, CT: International Universities Press, 1966.

------. "Indications for Child Analysis (1945)" in *The Psychoanalytic Treatment of Children: Lectures and Essays.* NY: Schoken Books, 1964.

------. *Introduction to the Technic of Child Analysis.* Classics in Child Development edition. NY: Arno Press, 1975.

Freud, Anna and Dorothy T. Burlingham. *War and Children.* Medical War Books. NY: Ernst Willard, 1943.

Freud, Sigmund. "An Autobiographical Study." *The Freud Reader.* Edited by Peter Gay. NY: Norton, 1995: 28-29.

------. *Beyond the Pleasure Principle.* Edited by Ernest Jones. Trans. C. J. M. Hubback. USA: Barnes & Noble, Inc. 2006.

------. *Totem and Taboo. The Basic Writings of Sigmund Freud.* Edited and translated by A. A. Brill. NY: The Modern Library, 1938, renewed 1966: 807-930.

------. *The Interpretation of Dreams* (1900). *The Basic Writings of Sigmund Freud.* Edited and translated by A. A. Brill. NY: The Modern Library, 1938, renewed 1966: 179-549.

Gackenbach, Jayne. "Electronic Media and Lucid-Control Dreams: Morning After Reports." *Dreaming: Journal of the Association for the Study of Dreams* 19.1 (March 2009): 1-6.

------. "Video Game Play and Lucid Dreams: Implications for the Development of Consciousness." *Dreaming: Journal of the Association for the Study of Dreams* 16.2 (June 2006): 96-110.

Gackenbach, Jayne and Arielle Boyes. "Social Media Versus Gaming Associations with Typical and Recent Dreams." *Dreaming: Journal of the Association for the Study of Dreams* 24.3 (September 2014): 182-202.

Gay, Peter. *Freud: A Life for Our Time.* NY: W. W. Norton, 1998.

------. *Reading Freud: Explorations & Entertainments*. New Haven, CT: Yale University Press, 1990.

George, Allison. "Are You Thinking What I'm Thinking…." *New Scientist* 220.2944 (23 November 2013): 36-40.

Germain, Anne et al. "Increased Mastery Elements Associated with Imagery Rehearsal Treatment for Nightmares in Sexual Assault Survivors with PTSD." *Dreaming: Journal of the Association for the Study of Dreams* 14.4 (December 2004): 195-206.

Gimbutas, Marija. *The Language of the Goddess*. San Francisco, CA: HarperSanFrancisco, 1989.

Giskin, Howard. "Dreaming the Seven-Colored Flower: Eastern and Western Approaches to Dreams in Chinese Folk Literature." *Asian Folklore Studies* 63.1 (2004): 79-94.

Goelet, Ogden, Jr. "Commentary." *The Egyptian Book of the Dead: The Book of Going Forth by Day*. Trans. Raymond Faulkner. San Francisco: Chronicle Books, 1998: 142.

Grunstein, Ronald. "Endocrine Disorders." *Principles and Practice of Sleep Medicine*. Edited by Kryger, Roth, and Dement. Canada: Elsevier, 2011: 1435-41.

Guilleminault, Christian et al. "Sleepwalking, a Disorder of NREM Sleep Instability. *Sleep Medicine* 7.2 (March 7, 2006): 163-70.

Gustafson, Fred. *Dancing Between Two Worlds: Jung and the Native American Soul*. NJ: Paulist Press, 1997.

Hall, James. *Jungian Dream Interpretation: A Handbook of Theory and Practice*. Canada: Inner City Books, 1983.

Hall, C. and V. J. Nordby. *A Primer of Jungian Psychology*. Canada: Mentor Books, 1973.

Heller, H. Craig, M.D. *Secrets of Sleep Science: From Dreams to Disorders*. The Great Courses, DVD online Stanford University Seminar. VA: The Teaching Company, 2013.

Hoffman, Curtiss. "Dumuzi's Dream: Dream Analysis in Ancient Mesopotamia." *Dreaming: Journal of the Association for the Study of Dreams* 14.4 (December 2004): 240-51.

Hoffner, Harry, Jr. "Ancient Views of Prophecy and Fulfillment: Mesopotamia and Asia Minor." *JETS* 30.3 (September 1987): 257-65.

Holm, Tom. *Strong Hearts and Wounded Souls: Native American Veterans of the Vietnam War.* Texis: University of Texas Press, Austin, 1996.

Holzinger, Brigitte, Stephen LaBerge, and Lynne Levitan. "Psychophysiological Correlates of Lucid Dreaming." *Dreaming: Journal of the Association for the Study of Dreams* 16.2 (June 2006): 88-95.

Hughes, Donald J. "A History of Dream Interpretation in Western Civilization from the Earliest Times Through the Middle Ages." *Dreaming* Impact Factor: 0.84 10.1 (February 2000): 7-18.

Hunter, Philip. "To Sleep, Perchance to Live: Sleeping is Vital for Health, Cognitive Function, Memory, and Long Life." *European Molecular Biology Organization Reports* 9.11 (November 2008): 1070-73.

Irwin, Lee. "Cherokee Healing: Myth, Dreams, and Medicine." *American Indian Quarterly* 16.2 (Spring 1992): 237-57.

Javaheri, Shahrokh. "Sleep and Cardiovascular Disease: Present and Future." *Principles and Practice of Sleep Medicine.* Edited by Kryger, Roth, and Dement. Canada: Elsevier, 2011: 1349-52.

Johnston-Saint, P. "An Outline of the History of Medicine in India. *Journal of the Royal Society of Arts* (12 July 1929): 843-870.

Jung, Carl Gustav. *The Archetypes and the Collective Unconscious.* Trans. Hull, R.F.C. NJ: Princeton University Press (Bollingen Series XX), 1959.

------. *Dreams,* 1st ed. 1974. Hull, R.F.C., trans. Shamdasani, Sonu. NJ: Princeton University Press (Bollingen Series XX), 2011.

------. *Jung: Analytical Psychology.* NY: Routledge, 2014.

------. *Man and His Symbols.* NY: Anchor Press, Doubleday, 1964.

------. *Memories, Dreams, Reflections* (revised ed.). Edited by Aniela Jaffe, Aniela, Richard Winston, and Clara Winston. NY: Vintage Books Edition, 1989.

------. *Psyche & Symbol: A Selection from the Writings of C.G. Jung.* Edited by Violet S. Laszlo. NY: Doubleday, 1958.

------. "The Meaning Of Psychology for Modern Man." *Civilization in Transition* in *The Collected Works of C.G. Jung.* Translated by R .F. C. Hull. (Bollingen Series XX) X, par. 304-305. NJ: Princeton University Press, 1970.

------. *The Red Book* (1930). Edited by Sonu Shamdasani, ed. and trans. Mark Kyburz and John Peck. NY: W. W. Norton: 2009.

Kasser, Rodlophe, et al., eds. *The Gospel of Judas from Codex Ichacos.* Washington, D.C.: National Geographic Society, 2006.

Kemp, Christopher. "Walking with Cavemen." *New Scientist* 220. 2948 (21 December 2013): 64-66.

Klein, Melanie. *Love, Guilt and Reparation & Other Works.* NY: Delta Books, 1975.

------. *The Psychoanalysis of Children.* Translated by Alix Strachey. NY: Delta Books, 1975.

Knudson, Roger M. "Anorexia Dreaming: A Case Study." *Dreaming: Journal of the Association for the Study of Dreams* 16.1 (March 2006): 43-52.

Kuiken, Don et al. "The Influence of Impactful Dreams on Self-Perceptual Depth and Spiritual Transformation." *Dreams: Journal of the Association for the Study of Dreams* 16.4 (December 2006): 258-79.

Lawrence, Christopher. "The Healing Serpent—The Snake in Medical Iconography." The Sir Thomas and Lady Dixon Memorial Lecture, posted on *PubMed Central,* online journal of U. S. National Institutes of Health 47.2 (1978): 134-40. Accessed 25 September 2014.

Levine Bar-Yoseph, Talia and Jay Levin. "Gestalt in the New Age," in *Gestalt Therapy: Advances in Theory and Practice.* Edited by Talia Levine Bar-Yoseph. NY: Routledge, 2012: 1-12.

Lincoln, Jackson Steward. *The Dream in Primitive Cultures.* NY: Johnson Reprint Corporation, 1970.

Lopes, M. C., M. A. Quera-Salva, and C. Guilleminault. "Non-REM Sleep Instability in Patients with Major Depressive Disorder: Subjective Improvement of Non-REM Sleep Instability with Treatment (Agomelatine)," *Sleep Medicine* 9.1 (December 9, 2007): 33-41.

Lowenstein, Tom and Piers Vitebsky. *Mother Earth, Father Sky: Native American Myth. Myth and Mankind.* London: Duncan Baird Publishers, 1997.

Lowis, Michael J. "Dreams and Their Relation to Physical and Mental Well-being." *The Journal of Social, Political, and Economic Studies* 35.3 (Fall 2010): 366-380.

MacFarlance, James G. and Harvey Moldofsky. "Fibromyalgia and Chronic Fatigue Syndromes." *Principles and Practice of Sleep Medicine.* Edited by Kryger, Roth, and Dement. Canada: Elsevier, 2011: 1422-34.

Marshack, Alexander. *The Roots of Civilization.* NY: Moyer Bell, 1991.

McClennon, James. "Shamanic Healing, Human Evolution, and the Origin of Religion." *Journal for the Scientific Study of Religion* 36.3 (1997): 345-54.

McWilliams, Nancy. *Psychoanalysis Diagnosis: Understanding Personality Structure in the Clinical Process.* NY: The Guilford Press, 1994.

Means, Stewart. "Ancient Healing and the Modern Mind." *The Journal of Religion* 5.1 (January 1925): 67-84.

Mednick, Sarah. *What are Dreams? Inside the Sleeping Brain.* Interview in Nova documentary. Edited by Jamie Effros, et al. Directed by Charles Colville and Sarah Holt. PBS Productions, 2009.

Mellman, Thomas A. and Wilfred R. Pigeon. "Dreams and Nightmares in Posttraumatic Stress Disorder." *Principles and Practice of Sleep Medicine.* Edited by Kryger, Roth, and Dement. Canada: Elsevier, 2011: 613-19.

Morris, Desmond. *The Naked Ape.* NY: Dell Publishing, 1969.

Nielson, Paula A. "The Rod of Asclepius and the Caduceus Symbols: Ancient Greek Snake Symbolism of Healing and Medicine." Online posting. https://suite.io/paula-i-nielson/37wd2dg (accessed 11 September 2014).

Nishimoto, Shinji et al. "Reconstructing Visual Experiences from Brain Activity Evoked by Natural Movies." *Current Biology* 21.19 (October 11, 2011): 1641-46.

Ong, Roberto Keh. *The Interpretation of Dreams in Ancient China.* Masters of Art Thesis, University of British Columbia in *Retrospective Theses and Dissertations,* 1919-2007 collection. Vancouver, B.C., May 1981.

Pace-Schott, E. F. "The Neurobiology of Dreaming." In *Principles and Practice of Sleep Medicine.* Edited by Kryger, Roth, and Dement. Canada: Elsevier, 2011: 563-75.

Perls, Frederick. *Gestalt Therapy Verbatim.* ME: Gestalt Journal Press, 1992.

Pettis, Jeffrey B. "Earth, Dream, and Healing: The Integration of *Materia* and Psyche in the Ancient World." *Journal of Religion and Health* 45.1 (Spring 2006): 113-29.

Phillips, Russell E., III and Kenneth I. Pargament. "The Sanctification of Dreams: Prevalence and Implications." *Dreaming: Journal of the Association for the Study of Dreams* 12.3 (September 2002): 141-53.

Picchioni, Dante et al. "Nightmares as a Coping Mechanism for Stress." *Dreaming: Journal of the Association for the Study of Dreams* 12.3 (September 2002): 155-69.

"PTSD: National Center for PTSD." U.S. Department of Veterans Affairs. 26 August 2014. http://www.ptsd.va.gov/ (accessed 19 September 2014.

Revonsuo, Antii. *What are Dreams? Inside the Sleeping Brain.* Interview in Nova documentary. Edited by Jamie Effros, et al. Directed by Charles Colville and Sarah Holt. PBS Productions, 2009.

Roberts, Jan, C. J. Lennings, and R. Heard. "Nightmares, Life Stress, and Anxiety: An Examination of Tension Reduction." *Dreaming: Journal of the Association for the Study of Dreams* 19.1 (March 2009): 17-29.

Sabini, Meredith. "Dreams: In Sickness and in Health." *Dreamtime* 30.2 (Spring 2013): 6-9.

Shakespeare, William. *The Complete Works of Shakespeare.* Edited by David Bevington. NJ: Pearson Education, 2004.

Shlain, Leonard. *The Alphabet Versus the Goddess: The Conflict Between Word and Image.* NY: Viking, 1998.

Shushan, Gregory. "Greek and Egyptian Dreams in Two Ptolemaic Archives: Individual and Cultural Layers of Meaning." *Dreaming: Journal of the Association for the Study of Dreams* 16.2 (June 2006): 129-42.

Siegel, Alan B. "Children's Dreams and Nightmares: Emerging Trends in Research." *Dreaming: Journal of the Association for the Study of Dreams* 15.3 (September 2005): 147-54.

Spotnitz, Hyman. *Modern Psychoanalysis of the Schizophrenic Patient: Theory of the Technique.* NY: Human Sciences Press, 1985.

Stickgold, Robert. *What are Dreams? Inside the Sleeping Brain.* Interview in Nova documentary. Edited by Jamie Effros, et al. Directed by Charles Colville and Sarah Holt. PBS Productions, 2009.

Stone, Merlin. *When God Was a Woman.* NY: Harcourt Brace, 1976.

Struthers, Roxanne. "The Lived Experience of Ojibwa and Cree Women Healers." *Journal of Holistic Nursing* 18.2 (September 2000): 261-79.

Tedlock, Barbara. "Divination as a Way of Knowing: Embodiment, Visualization, Narrative, and Interpretation." *Folklore* 112.2 (October 2001): 189-97.

------. "The Role of Dreams and Visionary Narratives in Mayan Cultural Survival." *Ethos* 20.4 (December 1992): 453-76.

Thilmany, Jean. "Next-Day Dreams." *Mechanical Engineering* 134.3 (March 2012): 18.

Tucker, Michael. *Dreaming with Open Eyes: The Shamanic Spirit in Twentieth Century Art and Culture.* CA: Aquarian/Thorsons, 1992.

Ullman, Montague. "Basic Dream Work—an Objective Comparison of Dream Groups & Therapy." *Dream Network Journal of the Exploration of Dreams,* 9.1 (Winter 1990). http://www.siivola.org/monte/papers-grouped/uncopyrighted/Dreams/Basic-Dream.Work.htm (accessed 13 April 2013).

------. "Dream Metaphor and *Psi.*" *Research in Parapsychology.* Edited by R. A. White and R.S. Brougton. Metuchen, NJ: Scarecrow Press, 1983: 138-52.

------. "Dream Work and the General Public." Presented at The Association for the Study of Dreams Conference III (June 23-29). Ottawa, Ontario, Canada. http://www.siivola.org/monte/papers-grouped/uncopyrighted/Dreams/Dream-Work-and-the-General-Public.htm (accessed 17 April 2013).

Ullman, Montague, Stanley Krippner, and Allan Vaughan. *Dream Telepathy.* NY: Macmillan Publishing, 1973.

Van den Bulck. "Media Use and Dreaming: The Relationship Among Television Viewing, Computer Game Play, and Nightmares or Pleasant Dreams." *Dreaming: Journal of the Association for the Study of Dreams* 14.1 (March 2004): 43-49.

Van den Daele, Leland. "Direct Interpretation of Dreams: Neuropsychology." *The American Journal of Psychoanalysis,* 56, 3 (Sep. 1996): 253-268.

Van der Horst, ed. *Persuasion and Dissuasion in Early Christianity, Ancient Judaism, and Hellenism.* Leuven, Belgium: Peeters Publishing, 2003.

Varela, Francisco, ed. *Sleeping, Dreaming, and Dying: An Exploration of Consciousness With The Dalai Lama.* MA: Wisdom Publications, 1997.

Vedfelt, Ole. *The Dimensions of Dreams: From Freud and Jung to Boss, Perls, and REM—a Comprehensive Sourcebook.* Tindall, Kenneth, trans. NY: Fromm International. 1998.

Verrier, Richard L. and Murray A. Mittleman. "Sleep-Related Cardiac Risk." *Principles and Practice of Sleep Medicine.* Edited by Kryger, Roth, and Dement. Canada: Elsevier, 2011: 1253-62.

Von Franz, M. –L. "The Process of Individuation." *Man and His Symbols.* Edited by Carl G. Jung. NY: Anchor Press, Doubleday, 1964: 158-229.

Walde, Christine. "Illness and Its Metaphors in Artemidorous' *Oneirocritica:* A Negative List." *Dreams, Healing, and Medicine in Greece: from Antiquity to the*

Present. Edited by Steven M. Oberhelman. England: Ashgate Publishing, Ltd., 2013: 129-60.

Walsh, James K., William C. Dement, and David F. Dinges. "Sleep Medicine, Public Policy, and Public Health." *Principles and Practice of Sleep Medicine.* Edited by Kryger, Roth, and Dement. Canada: Elsevier, 2011: 716-24.

Wayman, Alex. "Significance of Dreams in India and Tibet." *History of Religions* 7.1 (August 1967): 1-12.

Wilcox, Robert A. and Emma M. Whitham. "The Symbol of Modern Medicine: Why One Snake is More than Two." *Annals of Internal Medicine* 238.8 (15 April 2003): 673-7.

Williams, Nathan W. "Greek ASKLEPIOS, Latin AESCULAPIUS (or Asculapius) Roman God of Medicine." *JAMA* 281 (1999): 475.

Wordsworth, William. "Intimations of Immortality." *Poems in Two Volumes, vol. 2.* Amazon Digital Book Series (23 March 2011): Kindle, n.p. (accessed 23 August 2014).

------. "The World is Too Much With Us." *Poems in Two Volumes, vol. 2.* Amazon Digital Book Series (23 March 2011): Kindle, n.p. (accessed 23 August 2014).

Xie, Lulu, et al. "Sleep Drives Metabolite Clearance from the Adult Brain." *Science* 382.6156 (October 2013): 373-77.

Zimmer, Heinrich. *Philosophies of India.* Editied by Joseph Campbell. Bollingen Series XXVI. NJ: Princeton University Press, 1974.

CREDITS

Grateful acknowledgment is extended to the following for permission to reproduce previously printed photos, figures and illustrations:

Figure 1. *Venus of Laussel,* carved limestone block on rock shelter, c. 20,00-18,000 B.C.E. picture of original kept in Bordeaux museum, France. Photo 120 (talk/contribs), oeuvre don't Pauteur est mort depuis environ 25 000 ans, own work, wikipedia Creative Commons Attribution 3.0 Unported (https://creativecommons.org/licenses/by/3.0/deed.en) license.

Figure 2 Female Reproductive System—Anterior View. Mikael Haggstrom, own work, Commons, CC0 1.0 https://commons.wikimedia.org/w/ index.php?title+ File:Female_reproductive_system-interior_view.svg&oldid=156001592)

Figure 3 Shaman,Bison, Lascaux Caves—Prehistoric Paintings. I, Peter80, self -made, wikipedia Creative Commons Attribution-Share Alike 2.5 Generic (https://creativecommons.org/licenses/by-sa/2.5deed.en), 2.0 Generic (https://creativecommons.org/licenses/by-sa/2.0/deed.en) and 1.0 Generic (https://creativecommons.org/licenses/by-sa/1.0/deed.en) license.

Figure 4 Anantasayi Vishnu Deogargh. Bob King (http://flickr.com/photos/16406105@N00), wikipedia Creative Commons Attribution 2.0 Generic (https://creativecommons.org/licenses/by/2.0/deed.en) license.

Figure 5 Nataraja The Lord of Dance from Thanjavur Palace. Mullookkaaran, own work, wikipedia Creative Commons Attribution-Share Alike 4.0 International (https://creativecommons.org/licenses/by-sa/4.0/deed.en) license.

Figure 6 Om [AUM] symbol. Rugby471 (talk/contribs), (https://commons.wikimedia.org/wiki/File:Om_symbol.svg.

Cover/back cover Art, Constance Mayer, *The Dream of Happiness* (1819) Louvre Museum, public domain, wikipedia commons, Micowkin, http://1bp.blogspot.com/-BFHKmkp4s/T8Ku948QOO!/AAAAAAAAA9w/Ba Lamartimiere-Dream-of-Happiness-ART 149287.jpg/Author.

Grateful acknowledgment is extended to the following for permission to reproduce printed text:

Excerpts from Montague Ullman, "Dream, Metaphor and Psi," in R.A. White and R.S. Broughtn, eds. *Research in Parapsychology*, Metuchen, NJ: Scarecrow Press, 1983, imprint of Rowman & Littlefield, MD.

Excerpts from *Principles and Practice of Sleep Medicine, 5th ed.*, 2011 (ISBN 9781416066453), Kryger at al., eds., text and excerpts amounting to 550 words reprinted by permission of Elsevier Ltd., Oxford OX5 IGB, UK.

Excerpts from OleVedfelt, *The Dimensions of Dreams: From Freud and Jung to Boss, Perls, and REM—a Comprehensive Sourcebook* (1998), p.288 (19 words), p. 290 (54 words), p. 291 (38 words), p. 292 (27 words). Tindall, Kenneth, trans. reprinted with permission from Jessica Kingsley Publishers, Ltd. (London, NI 9JB).

Several excerpts [pp.1-105: 1092 words] from *ALL ABOUT DREAMS* by GAYLE DELANEY. Copyright © 1998 by Gayle Delaney, Ph.D. Reprinted by permission of HarperCollins Publishers.